Christian Social Witness

The New
Church's Teaching Series,
Volume 10

Christian
Social Witness

Harold T. Lewis

COWLEY PUBLICATIONS
Cambridge · Boston
Massachusetts

The title *The Church's Teaching Series* is used by permission of the Domestic and Foreign Missionary Society. Use of the series title does not constitute the Society's endorsement of the content of the work.

Library of Congress Cataloging-in-Publication Data:
Lewis, Harold T.,
    Christian Social Witness / Harold T. Lewis.
        p. cm.— (The new church's teaching series; v. 10)
    Includes bibliographical references.
    ISBN 1-56101-188-6 (alk. paper)
    1. Sociology, Christian. 2. Episcopal Church—Doctrines.
    3. Anglican Communion—Doctrines. I. Title. II. Series.
BX5930.2 .L49 2001
261.8′088′23—dc21   00—047392

Cynthia Shattuck and Gardiner Shattuck, editors; Vicki Black, copyeditor and designer.
Cover art: Icon of Jonathan Daniels, Episcopal Divinity School, Cambridge, Massachusetts

Scripture quotations are taken from *The New Revised Standard Version* of the Bible, © 1989, by the Division of Christian Education of the National Council of the Churches of Christ in the United States of America. Used by permission.

This book was printed by Transcontinental Printing in Canada on recycled, acid-free paper.

Cowley Publications
28 Temple Place • *Boston, Massachusetts 02111*
800-225-1534 • *www.cowley.org*

Table of Contents

   The Law Codes of the Hebrew Bible
   The Prophetic Witness
   Justice in the House of Israel
   The Psalms
   Justice in the New Testament
   The Church and Human Rights

   The Evangelicals
   The Christian Socialists
   The Tractarians and Anglo-Catholics
   Archbishop William Temple

   Slavery and the Civil War
   The Social Gospel
   The Civil Rights Movement

   The Lambeth Conference of 1998
   The Episcopal Church
   Implementing Economic Justice

The New Church's Teaching Series

Almost fifty years ago a series for the Episcopal Church called The Church's Teaching was launched with the publication of Robert Dentan's *The Holy Scriptures* in 1949. Again in the 1970s the church commissioned another church's teaching series for the next generation of Anglicans. Originally the series was part of an effort to give the growing postwar churches a sense of Anglican identity: what Anglicans share with the larger Christian community and what makes them distinctive within it. During that seemingly more tranquil era it may have been easier to reach a consensus and to speak authoritatively. Now, at the end of the twentieth century, consensus and authority are more difficult; there is considerably more diversity of belief and practice within the churches today, and more people than ever who have never been introduced to the church at all.

The books in this new teaching series for the Episcopal Church attempt to encourage and respond to the times and to the challenges that will usher out the old century and bring in the new. This new series differs from the previous two in significant ways: it has no official status, claims no special authority, speaks in a personal voice, and comes not out of committees but from scholars and pastors meeting and talking informally together. It assumes a different readership: adults who are not "cradle Anglicans," but who come from other religious traditions or from no tradition at all, and who want to know what Anglicanism has to offer.

As the series editor I want to thank E. Allen Kelley, former president of Morehouse Publishing, for initially inviting me to bring together a group of teachers and pastors who could write with learning and conviction about their faith. I am grateful both to him and to Morehouse for participating in the early development of the series.

Since those initial conversations there have been changes in the series itself, but its basic purpose has remained: to explore the themes of the Christian life through Holy Scripture, historical and contemporary theology, worship, spirituality, and social witness. It is our hope that all readers, Anglicans and otherwise, will find the books an aid in their continuing growth into Christ.

James E. Griffiss
Series Editor

Acknowledgments

To describe as "author" the one whose name appears on the title page of a book is somewhat misleading. Webster's first definition of "author" is "originator." The ideas that authors reduce to words do not, strictly speaking, originate with them but are the product of their experiences. This has certainly been true of this volume. My theology of social justice and my thoughts on the church's social witness owe a debt to the congregations with which I have been associated. In addition to St. Philip's, Brooklyn, New York, where I was baptized and confirmed and where my priestly vocation was nurtured, I have learned much from those with whom I have shared ministry at Santisima Trinidad, La Ceiba, Honduras; Little St. Mary's, Cambridge, England; St. Monica's, Washington; St. Luke's, New Haven; St. Mark's, Brooklyn; and Calvary, Pittsburgh, where I have been rector for the past four years. Taking seriously Archbishop William Temple's assertion that the church is the only institution that exists primarily for the benefit of those who are not its members, each of these parishes has seen its ministry as extending beyond the walls of the congregation.

To these parochial experiences must be added the decade I spent on the presiding bishop's staff at the national church headquarters in New York, where I was able to experience firsthand the challenges and frustrations inherent in attempting to raise the consciousness of the whole church on matters of social witness. Finally, at another level, I bring to this book the experience of being an African American, a member of a so-called minority group within both the Episcopal Church and society at large—an experience that has enabled me to look at the issue of social witness through a particular set of lenses.

I am grateful to my colleagues Richard Burnett, Richard Tolliver, and Jared Jackson; to Calvaryites Jim Bauerle and Alan Lewis; and to fellow authors Charles Hefling and Fredrica Thompsett for their helpful comments at various stages in the preparation of this manuscript. I also wish to thank Nancy and Milton Washington for providing me the refuge of their home on Martha's Vineyard, where much of this book was written. Thanks are owed as well to Ann Smith of the Office of Women's Ministries for providing documents from that office's archives and for directing me to additional sources of information.

To my wife, Claudette Richards Lewis, I give my deepest appreciation for her encouragement and insights, and above all for her willingness to put up with months of benign neglect as this book evolved from first draft to finished product. My most profound debt of gratitude goes to Cynthia Shattuck and James E. Griffiss for their timely advice, inspired guidance, gentle prodding, and consummate patience. They have been of invaluable help to me as this volume has taken shape.

This book is dedicated to my son, Justin Craig Lewis, in the hope that his and subsequent generations may truly know a church and a world in which men and women will "do justice, love mercy, and walk humbly with their God."

Christian Social Witness

Not only with our lips, but in our lives.
—The Book of Common Prayer, 72

This book on Christian social witness is among the later volumes of The New Church's Teaching Series not because it is less important than the study of scripture, church history, or prayer. Christian social witness is not a mere footnote to these foundations of our faith, but is an outgrowth of them. It is faith in action. It is what we do as a consequence of what we believe. The church, sometimes corporately and officially, sometimes through the actions of its individual members, makes choices, takes stands, and speaks out on issues affecting both its own life and the life of the society of which it is a constituent part. It does so because it is guided by its theology, by its understanding of scripture, and by its life of prayer. A church that makes no social witness is unimaginable because such witness is part and parcel of our job description as church.

We are everywhere reminded of the importance of social witness. Jesus, in the last sermon of his earthly ministry, challenges us with these words: "You will be my witnesses" (Acts 1:8). The apostle James seems especially keen on this point when he reminds us that "faith without works...is dead" (2:26) and that we should be "doers of the word and not merely hearers" (1:22). Our hymnody reinforces the idea. The familiar refrain of Mary Ann Thomson's great hymn, "O Zion, haste," speaks to it: "Publish glad tidings: tidings of peace, tidings of Jesus, redemption and release." And there is probably no more stirring call to social witness than the familiar words of George Duffield's hymn: "Stand up, stand up, for Jesus; the trumpet call obey." This theme, too, is beautifully expressed in *The Book of Common Prayer*, in the incomparable cadences of Archbishop Thomas Cranmer's General Thanksgiving:

> And, we beseech thee, give us that due sense of all thy mercies, that our hearts may be unfeignedly thankful; and that we show forth thy praise, not only with our lips, but in our lives, by giving up our selves to thy service, and by walking before thee in holiness and righteousness all our days. (BCP 71-72)

The term "social witness," however, connotes far more than rendering service to our fellow human beings. It conveys the idea of taking one's faith into the world, standing up for it, and, when necessary, suffering the consequences. The Greek word for "witness" is *marturion*, a public testimony of one's faith. This term gradually came to signify a person who witnessed even unto death: hence, our English word "martyr." "Social" emphasizes the arena in which that witness is made—that is, not safely ensconced with fellow Christians within the walls and stained glass windows of our parish churches, but in society at large. One postcommunion prayer makes it clear that witnessing to our faith should be seen as both benefit and consequence of receiving our Lord under the species of bread and wine: "And now, Father, send us out to do the work you have given us to do, to love and serve you as *faithful witnesses* of Christ our Lord" (BCP 366).

When it comes to social witness, Anglicanism in general and the Episcopal Church in particular have been unfairly caricatured. English bishops were once portrayed as aloof individuals holding court in their episcopal palaces, while parish clergy were lampooned as caring more about fishing and fox hunting than about praying. Episcopalians in this country have been referred to as "the landed gentry" or "the carriage trade." A book published in 1978 attempted to give academic credence to the cherished belief that the Episcopal Church is the denomination to join when climbing the proverbial social ladder.[1] The laity, both in the Church of England and in the Episcopal Church, have also been generally characterized as indifferent— as people who defined "outreach" (according to one wag) as "keeping others out of our reach"!

But we know that these stereotypical views have distorted the true picture. Indeed, as Gardiner Shattuck points out in his recent book, the Episcopal Church is "heir to a rich tradition of social Christianity that had influenced Anglicans in Britain and the United States" for several centuries.[2] F. D. Maurice, one of the most important Anglican theologians of the nineteenth century and a great proponent of Christian Socialism, emphasized God's engagement in the world through the incarnate Christ. Maurice and other Christian Socialists, such as Charles Gore and William Temple, were "incarnationalists." They believed that because God participated in the life of humankind through the birth, death, and resurrection of Jesus Christ, there could be no worldly activity that fell outside the concern of the church. This commitment was also embodied by followers of the Oxford Movement, who took their faith into the streets of the East End of London and founded parishes and religious orders to serve the poor. Christians live and move and have their being in the world. Since (as St. Paul admonishes the Romans) the Christian's task is to transform the world, the church recognizes no dichotomy between "sacred" and "secular."

It was largely to emphasize the connection between theology and social witness, between what the church believes and what it does, that the first Church's Teaching Series was written a half-century ago. In his volume, *The Episcopal Church and Its Work*, Professor Powel Mills Dawley of General Seminary described the church as the "conscience of society."[3] Bishop Stephen Bayne, in the volume called *Christian Living*, stressed that it is the responsibility of Christians to be involved in the political process in order to ensure that society conforms to God's will. The Episcopal Church has borne such witness institutionally through the establishment, for instance, of the Freedman's Commission following the Civil War and the General Convention Special Program in the late 1960s. The church has also acted through the prophetic witness of individuals, such as Mary Abbot Twing and Vida Scudder, pioneers in the women's movement; Charles Rainsford, whose parish (St. George's, New York) was a model for Christian outreach; and seminarian Jonathan Daniels, who became a witness unto death in the civil rights movement.

The principal question that arises as we examine these movements and individuals concerns the motivation of those who have contributed to the church's

social witness by standing on the side of the marginalized and oppressed. What standard did they claim?
What warranted their involvement or their interfer-
ence in society? The answer, I believe, is justice.

Justice is a concept that is inextricably woven into
the rich tapestry of Holy Scripture. At one level it suggests doing what is right, just, and pleasing in God's
sight. But as a biblical concept it also conveys a sense
of advocacy—of taking up the cause of groups who
for a variety of reasons (tribal, social, geographic,
racial, economic, or sexual) have been abused and
mistreated by those in power. "You trample on the
poor and take from them levies of grain," says the
prophet Amos. Therefore, though "you have built
houses of hewn stone, . . . you shall not live in them"
(5:11). Amos also makes it clear that even the most
beautiful worship is an affront to God, if worshipers
are not also champions of the oppressed: "I hate, I
despise your festivals. . . . Even though you offer me
your burnt offerings and grain offerings, I will not
accept them" (5:21).

Moreover, being a social witness and doing justice
are not simply *options* for those who "profess and call
themselves Christians" (BCP 815). They are in our "job
description," and they are part of the commitment we
make when we are incorporated into the body of
Christ through the sacrament of baptism. The cele-
brant asks, "Will you strive for justice and peace
among all people, and respect the dignity of every
human being?" And we answer, "I will, with God's
help" (BCP 305).

One might argue that living out this baptismal
covenant is more demanding, certainly more complex,
for Christians today than it was when the first
Church's Teaching Series was published. If that question had been part of the baptismal liturgy forty or

fifty years ago, what would phrases such as "all people" and "every human being" have conjured up? The average Episcopalian in those days might have imagined people in the "mission field" overseas as being part of that group. But would racial and ethnic minorities at home have come to mind, and if so, how would their "dignity" have been understood? Would that term have been associated somehow with the social position minorities were expected to occupy?

The poor would certainly have been considered, if only as an object of the church's largess, but the moral dilemmas created by oppressive third-world debt would not likely have entered the picture. In the 1950s, male dominance and privilege were such givens in our society, and gender-specific roles were so ingrained, that only a valiant few would have dared to describe women as an oppressed group. And most assuredly, for the overwhelming majority of churchgoers, homosexual persons would have been excluded from any group in which "the dignity of every human being" was recognized and acknowledged. Moreover, those who disagreed with the majority in that conformist era would surely have been loath to voice their opinions.

"New occasions teach new duties," wrote James Russell Lowell in an old hymn; "time makes ancient good uncouth." The demands of our baptismal covenant must be reexamined in light of the exigencies of a changing society. All of us must discern the ways in which we may render social witness, thereby exercising our respective ministries in the name of him who came "not to be served but to serve, and to give his life a ransom for many" (Matthew 20:28). I hope that the following pages will provide useful insights into the carrying out of this important exercise.

The Bible

Let justice roll down like waters,
and righteousness like an everflowing stream.

Amos 5:24

There is probably no canticle more familiar or beloved among Anglicans than the *Magnificat*, the Song of Mary appointed to be sung at the service of Evening Prayer. Great English composers like Stanford, Howells, and Byrd have placed these words from Luke's gospel (1:46-55) in beautiful and majestic musical settings—so beautiful that we may run the risk of missing the deep significance of those words. But we do not have to stretch the meaning of the text to see that it is a message of justice and liberation:

> He has mercy on those who fear him
> in every generation.
> He has shown the strength of his arm,
> he has scattered the proud in their conceit.
> He has cast down the mighty from their
>   thrones,
> and has lifted up the lowly.
> He has filled the hungry with good things,
> and the rich he has sent away empty.
>
> (BCP 119)

We should remember that Mary utters these words during the event Christians have come to call the Visitation—the occasion on which Mary (having obediently responded to the announcement of the angel that she would conceive in her womb and bear Jesus, the incarnate Lord) pays a call on her cousin Elizabeth, herself pregnant with John the Baptist. Mary's words are in response to Elizabeth's proclamation at their meeting, "Blessed is she who believed that there would be a fulfillment of what was spoken to her by the Lord" (Luke 1:45). Mary, who understands the meaning of Jesus' coming into the world, describes the radical implications of Jesus' ministry, a blueprint for which he himself would later give in his first sermon, delivered in the synagogue at Nazareth, where he begins, "The Spirit of the Lord is upon me, because he has anointed me to bring good news to the poor" (Luke 4:14-20).

We have an even deeper appreciation for the *Magnificat* when we learn that it is the transposition of a Hebrew poem based on the Song of Hannah. This song gives thanks to God for the birth of Samuel, the greatest of the judges of Israel, and signals an end to oppression for the downtrodden and weak (1 Samuel 2:1-10). The songs of Hannah and Mary illustrate in a poignant way that the theme of justice is found on virtually every page of the Bible. Both these hymns teach that God is a strong advocate of justice, and that all sinful values and structures upon which men and women have placed their hopes will eventually be overturned. For Hannah and for Mary, their sons are seen as pledges on the part of God that a new social order will soon be inaugurated. These hymns speak, moreover, of the existence of economic and political inequity, and they show how wealth all too often has a tendency to corrupt. Hannah and Mary believe that

God provides a corrective to such inequity. Hannah declares, "The Lord makes poor and makes rich; he brings low, he also exalts," while Mary says, "He has brought down the powerful from their thrones, and lifted up the lowly." It is no wonder that Thomas Hancock, a reform-minded minister of the nineteenth century, took delight in reminding his Church of England congregation that the *Magnificat* is a hymn whose theme is social revolution!

⮐ The Law Codes of the Hebrew Bible

Because of these texts, one might rightly argue that the theme of justice is critical for an understanding of all Holy Scripture. Theologian Maria Harris tells a story about a professor who, when asked to name the most important texts on justice from the Hebrew Bible, replied, "It is very difficult to do that. The entire Bible is about justice."[1]

The concept of justice is first found in the law codes of the Old Testament. The law codes are those parts of the Torah, the first five books of the Hebrew Bible, that contain prescriptions and proscriptions for the conduct of life. The three law codes are the Book of the Covenant (Exodus 20:22–23:33), the earliest of the codes and the only one written before the the time of the prophets; the Deuteronomic Code (Deuteronomy 12–26); and the Holiness Code (Leviticus 17–26), both of which existed in oral form before the prophets but were not written down until later. While the Book of the Covenant and the Holiness Code offer a few striking statements on the subject of justice, the Deuteronomic Code contains the most material on the just treatment of the poor of Israel.[2] Unlike the narratives of the prophets or the poetry of the psalms, the law codes promoting social justice are made up of simple, often pithy statements that lay down the rules of proper conduct.

These legal codes governing human relationships also contain commands that forbid oppressive actions, and they exhort those who would follow the law to offer positive deeds on behalf of the deprived. Justice for the oppressed was a key factor in maintaining the covenant relationship between God and Israel. Those people included in "the oppressed" are often, as in Exodus 22:21-24, the sojourner, the widow, and the fatherless. In regard to these groups, the Holiness Code goes further and demands that the sojourners and natives be governed by a single law. According to theologian Bruce Malchow, these commands "reveal high ethical sensitivity in not only providing total justice for people easily misused but also in calling for equality with and love toward them."[3] Such laws set the standard for social justice, predicated as they were on the beliefs that outsiders should not be beyond the reach of compassion, and that further, those who are without advocates have a particular claim on the mercy of those who do. This standard is one that provides the basis for teachings on social justice elsewhere in the Old Testament, particularly in the prophetic books and in the psalms.

One of the largest groups of law codes is comprised of those forbidding actions that might deprive the poor. Even a cursory study of these laws reveals their thoroughness and attention to detail, for the compilers of the laws seem to have been aware of virtually every circumstance that could present an opportunity to take advantage of the poor. Accordingly, there are laws prohibiting usury and laws about pledges for loans. Because a poor person might need a cloak for warmth, the garment had to be returned to its owner by sundown if used as a pledge for a loan

(Deuteronomy 24:12-13), while a widow's cloak could not be used as a pledge at all. There are several laws concerning measure, since it was not uncommon for the poor to be cheated in the marketplace. Not surprisingly, a large number of law codes have to do with prohibiting actions that perpetrated injustice in courts of law.

In addition to those laws forbidding behavior that would adversely affect the lot of the poor and deprived, other laws *prescribe* acts of justice to ensure their well-being and inclusion in the household. Leviticus 25:35-38 mandates that an Israelite must support a family member who falls into poverty by providing food, shelter, and loans without interest. Although most apoditic laws in the legal codes are simple do's and don'ts, occasionally a rationale for the existence of the law is given. In this case, those who would follow the law are reminded that they should extend compassion because the LORD God had extended compassion to them by bringing them out of slavery in Egypt and into the land of Canaan. The Lord was reminding them, in effect, not to forget their own history as an oppressed people. Still other laws call for gifts to be made to the poor, such as the provision that every third year the agricultural tithes normally used for cultic purposes were to be set aside for widows, orphans, and resident aliens (Deuteronomy 14:28-29).

Of these laws, those pertaining to the provision of jubilee—or a sabbatical year—are the most significant. Originating from an agricultural provision to allow the land to go fallow so that it might renew itself, the observation of jubilee developed into a way of providing food for the needy. Thus, we read in Exodus 23:10-11, "For six years you shall sow your land and gather in its yield; but the seventh year you shall let it rest and lie fallow, so that the poor of your people may eat." A significant further development of this practice was a provision for the canceling of debts in the seventh year, as well as releasing prisoners and bondservants (Leviticus 25). These provisions were made so that greater economic parity could exist between rich and poor. The legal codes recognized the fact that, left to their own devices, the rich would simply get richer at the expense of the poor. Providing a "bonus" every seven years approximated a leveling of the playing field and gave the poor an opportunity to extricate themselves from their impecunious lot. Indeed, as Maria Harris points out, "such a practice would have provided equity since the poor would have gained property and freedom from service without price."[4]

Because Jesus inaugurated his ministry with the declaration of a jubilee year by citing the words from the sixty-first chapter of Isaiah ("I will proclaim the year of the Lord's favor"), the concept of jubilee is extremely important for Christians as well. In recent years, moreover, most notably at the 1998 Lambeth Conference, Anglicans advocating the eradication of third-world debt have recommended that a year of jubilee be declared. At that time the developed nations would forgive the debts of developing countries—a crushing load that, given the compounding of interest, can never be repaid under the existing economic system.

Then, as now, the genius of the legal codes in general and of jubilee in particular is that they provide *practical* solutions to the problems of the poor. As we shall see, those engaged in Christian social witness today through economic incentive programs are concentrating on practical approaches that are devoid of pious platitudes. In the ancient world, the legal codes represented what could be called a holistic approach to the problem of the poor, as opposed to so many of the superficial approaches that have characterized programs for the poor in recent decades. The legal codes attempted to prevent the problem by prohibiting unjust acts toward the poor in the first place. They provided redress for the poor when they were wronged; they stimulated giving in an attempt to close the gap between rich and poor; and through jubilee they provided a kind of amnesty that gave the poor an additional opportunity to better their situation. Moreover, the codes were placed in a framework of compassion, gratitude for God's blessings, and an encouragement to emulate God's own actions on behalf of the poor. At a very basic level, the principle of jubilee describes what God desires for humanity, namely, an equitable distribution of resources and a curbing of the tendency to accumulate possessions.

～ The Prophetic Witness

Important as these law codes are in understanding the Old Testament witness, when we think of justice in the Hebrew scriptures we tend to recall most often the words of the prophets, where the most striking statements on social justice occur. Prophets are not, as is commonly believed, fortune-tellers or predictors of the future; they are people who read the signs of the times and interpret them for their people. "A prophet is a person," Harris writes, "who announces a message received through direct inspiration by a god and who speaks from the fringes of the religious institution." Because of their link with the deity, prophets also enjoy a relative autonomy from the dominant religious and political structures of their society. Thus, they never preach "a watered-down justice" but one that is "passionate, tempestuous, hotheaded, and most of all, immediately necessary."[5] And because the Hebrew prophets were eyewitnesses to the perpetration of injustices, their words were also marked by an unmistakable sense of indignation.

While all of the prophets addressed the issue of social justice, the ones who clearly had the most to say about this topic were Amos, Micah, Isaiah, and Jeremiah. Regardless of their background, they made the temple authorities feel uncomfortable. They were about the business of afflicting the comfortable and comforting the afflicted. Prophesying in the north during the eighth century, Amos had as his chief antagonist Amaziah, the temple priest who wanted to maintain the status quo. Amaziah told the prophet, "Go, flee away to the land of Judah, earn your bread there, and prophesy there; but never again prophesy at Bethel, for it is the king's sanctuary" (Amos 7:12). Speaking in contemporary terms, we could say that while Amaziah espoused civil religion, Amos championed civil rights.

It is not surprising, therefore, that we find in Amos perhaps the most well-known statement about justice found in the Old Testament: "Let justice roll down like waters, and righteousness like an everflowing stream" (5:24). In the verses that precede this one, God declares, "I despise your festivals, and I take no delight in your solemn assemblies. Even though you offer me your burnt offerings and grain offerings, I will not accept them" (vv. 21-22). Here God chastises his people for empty ritual as a substitute for righteousness, for worship is not only meaningless but also hypocritical and idolatrous if the worshipers do not execute justice. Amos exhorts his hearers that what is required of them is not to express devotion in the form of self-serving religious activities, but instead to inaugurate a new social order. This new order is described metaphorically as "an everflowing stream," cascading waters that never run dry, symbolic both of sufficiency and permanence. To stress his point, Amos observes that when the Israelites were in exile for forty years, no cereal offerings were offered to Yahweh; instead, their faithfulness revealed itself in many expressions of love toward one another.

In these passages Amos uses the Hebrew word *mispat*, meaning "justice," which has its roots in the idea of relationship, either among God's people or between humankind and God. *Mispat* can variously be translated as "judgment," "rights," "vindication," and "deliverance." It refers to the restoration of a situation or an environment that promotes equity and harmony in community. It is impossible for a solitary individual to be right or just—that would be like one hand clapping! A righteous person in Israel was one who preserved the peace and integrity of the community and fulfilled the demands of communal living. The idea of individuality as such does not figure prominently in the Old Testament. Rather, individuals are seen as members of tribes, members of families, inhabitants of cities. The ways in which they relate to each other, treat each other, honor (or dishonor) each other are seen as paramount. As John Donahue observes, "In contrast to modern individualism, the Israelite is in a world where 'to live' is to be united with others in a social context either by bonds of family or by covenant relationships"—king with people, judge with complainants, community with the resident alien, and everyone with God.[6]

One of the themes to which all the prophets addressed themselves was the disparity of resources between the rich and the poor. The prophets believed that this disparity existed primarily because the rich had stripped the poor of their possessions. The rich were so evil, in fact, that the prophets often depicted them as staying up at night to plot evil and then working out their mischief during the day. Thus Micah, another eighth-century prophet, could proclaim:

> Alas for those who devise wickedness
> and evil deeds on their beds!
> When the morning dawns, they perform it,
> because it is in their power.
> They covet fields, and seize them;
> houses, and take them away;
> they oppress householder and house,
> people and their inheritance. (Micah 2:1-2)

After stripping away the possessions of the poor, the rich also imposed taxes that the poor could not possibly pay, so that they were often forced to sell themselves or their children into slavery. As Amos said, the rich "sell the righteous for silver, and the needy for a pair of sandals" (2:6).

The poor, therefore, are not simply those without funds. They are those who are so far removed from the mainstream of society that they are unable to participate in its life. They are the outcasts of the house of Israel. Even those entrusted with protecting them were corrupt, offering no assistance to the downtrodden. Thus the prophet Ezekiel condemned the court at Jerusalem: "Its officials within it are like wolves tearing the prey, shedding blood, destroying lives to get dishonest gain" (22:27). Isaiah addressed the same problem when he said that God "expected justice [mispat], but saw bloodshed [mispah]; righteousness [sedeqah], but heard a cry [se'aqah]" (5:7). The implications for us today are similarly striking. Like the poor of ancient Israel, members of our nation's underclass are virtually hopeless, since they have access neither to power nor even to the means of a livelihood.

But the prophets did not stop at merely lamenting the lot of the poor and condemning those responsible for their situation. They also offered hope to the poor, a hope grounded in the belief held by liberation theologians today that God himself identifies with the poor and has a "preferential option for the oppressed."[7] It is because of this relationship with the poor that Yahweh established a covenant with the whole house of Israel. This covenant is envisioned by the prophet Hosea as a "marriage" in which God is betrothed to Israel:

> I will abolish the bow, the sword, and war from the land; and I will make you lie down in safety. And I will take you for my wife forever; I will take you for my wife in righteousness and in justice, in steadfast love, and in mercy. (Hosea 2:18-19)

In this way, Yahweh seals the covenant made with Israel on Mount Sinai. This betrothal, it should be noted, is further characterized by the fact that the "husband" Yahweh promises to remove every vestige of conflict and war and to establish righteousness, justice, love, and mercy—surely good attributes for any marriage.

∾ Justice in the House of Israel

As regards the nature of the covenant relationship between Yahweh and the people of God, it must be remembered that in a patriarchal society the well-being of the whole family depended upon the wealth and social standing of the *paterfamilias*, the male head of household from whom devolved all wealth, property, and status. The just person was one who cared for those with no standing, namely the fatherless and the widow. Such concern might require that the just person go the proverbial second mile and become an advocate for the marginalized in court: "Speak out for those who cannot speak, for the rights of all the destitute. Speak out, judge righteously, defend the rights of the poor and needy" (Proverbs 31:8-9).

But while dedication to the welfare of one's community was central to the concerns of the righteous, the law also expected that they would extend justice to outsiders, both strangers and guests: "You shall also love the stranger, for you were strangers in the land of Egypt" (Deuteronomy 10:19). No one, therefore, was outside the reach of the just person's benevolence and compassion. An example of the extent of God's benevolence to outsiders is illustrated in Isaiah 56:5, where Yahweh declares that even faithful eunuchs will receive "in my house and within my walls, a monument and a name better than sons and daughters. I will give them an everlasting name that shall not be cut off." Since those who had been emasculated were excluded by law from the assembly of the Lord, this is an especially shocking statement. In a society whose members were bidden to "increase and multiply," in which children were considered one's riches and in which wealth and property were handed down to rightful heirs, the declaration that eunuchs' memorials would be superior to those of legitimate heirs was extremely radical.

This is a pivotal concept to which we shall return throughout this book as we examine the phenomenon of social witness. Ministry to those identified as "outsiders," "strangers," "aliens," and "others" (often defined according to race, gender, or sexual orientation) is the truest measure of the church's commitment to justice. The church, as Archbishop William Temple once said, exists primarily for the benefit of those who are not its members. This was certainly the intention of Jesus, who revealed himself not merely to the house of Israel, but to the Gentiles as well. Thus the prophets challenged the rich and powerful to amend their ways and carry out the simple duty of every just person: "What does the Lord require of you but to do justice, and to love kindness, and to walk humbly with your God?" (Micah 6:8).

There is another understanding of the concept of justice in the Old Testament that is crucial to our grasp of Christian social witness. The scriptures teach that the oppressed are deemed righteous by God *because* of their oppression. To put it another way, the righteous are not only those who actually fulfill the demands of a relationship with God and other human beings, but also those whose rights to such relationships have been *taken away.* This conviction originated in the fact that the people of Israel were oppressed and deprived of their rights during the period of bondage in Egypt. The introduction to the ten commandments in the book of Exodus grounds all law in the historical act that gave birth to Israel: "I am the LORD your God, who brought you out of the land of Egypt, out of the house of slavery" (20:2). Since the victims of those who were evil were, like the Israelites, considered just because of their deprivation, it was the duty of those who were just because of their relationship with God to defend the cause of the oppressed in their midst. This idea is eloquently expressed in the psalms, which often characterize God as the refuge of prisoners and all who are oppressed.

∼ The Psalms

The psalms, which play such a significant part in Anglican worship, contain some of the Bible's most poignant statements about this aspect of justice. Even a cursory study of the psalms reveals that their authors not only were passionate about justice, but also possessed deep insights into the reasons for the existence of injustices and the motivation of those who oppress. Oppressors are described as people who are arrogant, smug, and believe themselves to be beyond God's judgment. They have forgotten about God and do not take into account God's presence and activity on behalf of the poor:

> In the pride of their countenance the wicked
> say, "God will not seek it out";
> all their thoughts are, "There is no God." . . .
> Your judgments are on high,
> out of their sight. (Psalm 10:4-5)

This preoccupation with the accumulation of wealth on the part of the wicked can be seen throughout the psalms. Psalm 10 speaks vividly of the wicked rich who are always waiting to ambush the poor:

> In hiding places they murder the innocent.
> Their eyes stealthily watch for the helpless;
> they lurk in secret like a lion in its covert;
> they lurk that they may seize the poor;
> they seize the poor and drag them off
> in their net. (Psalm 10:8-9)

Using this figurative language, the psalm suggests that the "murder" of the needy can take place through unjust legal proceedings that deprive them of their livelihood. Passages such as this are also germane to our understanding of social witness today because they speak so clearly to the contemporary issue of economic injustice. The scriptures remind us of the imbalance of power that exists in our society. The poor today often have little economic or legal recourse, and they tend to find themselves in a state of continuous deprivation.

Even while analyzing and condemning the motives of the wicked rich, the psalms hold out hope for the poor. Some of the wisdom psalms point to the fact that wealth is fleeting and temporal:

> Do not be afraid when some become rich,
> > when the wealth of their houses increases.
> For when they die they will carry nothing
> > away; their wealth will not go down
> > after them. (Psalm 49:16-17)

Others directly express the plight of the poor, who cry out to God for help and deliverance (70:5), while still others reassure them that God will indeed punish the wicked (10:12-15). But it is Psalm 146 that best sums up the psalmist's expectations of Yahweh's actions on behalf of the oppressed. God is the one

> who executes justice for the oppressed;
> > who gives food to the hungry.
> The LORD sets the prisoners free;
> > the LORD opens the eyes of the blind.
> The LORD lifts up those who are bowed down;
> > the LORD loves the righteous.
> The LORD watches over the strangers;
> > he upholds the orphan and the widow,
> but the way of the wicked he brings to ruin.
> > > > (Psalm 146:7-9)

As we have already seen, the Hebrew Bible understands justice not simply in terms of the relationship between God and the people of Israel, but also in terms of the relationships among the people of God. Indeed,

God uses Israel to execute justice, and the psalms speak often of the role of men and women as God's agents in helping the poor. The king, who was thought to be endowed with divine attributes and wielded considerable power, was expected to play a unique role as advocate. In Psalm 72, which is a hymn to the king's righteousness and sense of justice, the king himself is the one who

> delivers the needy when they call,
>> the poor and those who have no helper.
> He has pity on the weak and the needy,
>> and saves the lives of the needy.
> From oppression and violence he redeems
>> their life;
> and precious is their blood in his sight.
>> (Psalm 72:12-14)

The message of the psalms is timeless, and their poetry speaks to the human condition, both ancient and contemporary. They accurately describe the injustices that beset society; they condemn those who perpetrate them, and they enlist the aid of God and of God's people to redress them. In this same way the concept of justice permeates the entire Old Testament. God, in fulfilling the divine commitment to maintain a covenant relationship with the people of Israel, is constant in its administration. God intervenes, saves, forgives, restores. For our part, we human beings, though fallible, are bidden to follow the divine example in our relationship both with God and with all humankind. God's justice, which we emulate and attempt to mirror in our own ministries, must therefore be constant, unstinting, and unbridled. Justice is not capricious, something to be exercised at whim, but it undergirds and characterizes the actions of the people of God "at all times and in all places."

～ Justice in the New Testament

When we turn to the New Testament, we see that it is Jesus, in whom God has reestablished the covenant relationship, who builds upon and expands the theme of justice. The Incarnation is the event through which God assumes not only human flesh, but also the human condition.[8] Predating the gospels, Paul's epistles were the first New Testament writings to reflect theologically on this fact. God's solidarity with humanity as made manifest in Christ is celebrated in the great incarnational hymn in Paul's letter to the Philippians. Jesus

> did not regard equality with God as something to be exploited, but emptied himself, taking the form of a slave, being born in human likeness. And being found in human form, he humbled himself and became obedient to the point of death. (Philippians 2:6-8)

Underscoring God's identification with the poor, Paul also writes in 1 Corinthians (in words reminiscent of the *Magnificat*):

> God chose what is foolish in the world to shame the wise; God chose what is weak in the world to shame the strong; God chose what is low and despised in the world, things that are not, to reduce to nothing things that are. (1 Corinthians 1:27-28)

And this theme is developed even more explicitly in Paul's second letter to the Corinthians, where he reminds his readers that Jesus, "though he was rich, yet for your sakes he became poor, so that by his poverty you might become rich" (8:9).

The gospel of John expands this incarnational theme to its fullest extent; the entire gospel can be described as a theological treatise on the Incarnation. Its prologue speaks of Jesus as *logos*, the Word, who "came to what was his own, and his own people did not accept him" (1:11). The rest of the gospel is largely a story about those who *did* receive him and to whom he ministered—outcasts, like the woman of Samaria, and those whom the Hebrew Bible regarded as strangers and aliens.

Emphasis on Jesus' ministry to aliens and outcasts is not unique to John's gospel, however. In his dialogue with the young lawyer in Luke's gospel, for example, Jesus tells the well-known parable of the Good Samaritan (10:29-37). Whenever I read or hear this parable, I am reminded of a question I posed to the schoolchildren at Holy Trinity Church in La Ceiba, Honduras, where I began my ordained ministry. "Why didn't the priest stop to help the man on the side of the road?" I asked. A third-grade boy replied: "He was on his way to say mass, and didn't want to get his hands dirty." This was, of course, an accurate and theologically insightful answer, since in Jewish law, touching a dead body would defile the priest's hands and make him unsuitable to offer sacrifice. The point Jesus makes in this parable is that while the priest was legally justified in ignoring the plight of the man beaten and left for dead, the biblical commitment to mercy, compassion, and justice demanded that he minister to him regardless. Jesus drives the point home by making a hero out of the Samaritan, whom Jews considered to be ritually unclean and with whom they had no dealings. Since the idea of a "good Samaritan" was an oxymoron in Jesus' time, his listeners were shocked to learn that "neighbor" encompassed anyone in need, not merely those of one's own household, race, tribe, or social class.

Several of Luke's other parables similarly address the issue of justice. The parable of the rich man and the beggar Lazarus (16:19-31) instructs us in the moral obligation to care for the poor in our midst. The parable of the Pharisee and the publican is reminiscent of Amos: it points to the emptiness and inefficacy of worship when it is not accompanied by compassion toward our fellow human beings (18:9-14). And in perhaps the most beloved of parables, the prodigal son, Jesus makes it clear that he has come to reclaim the least, the lost, and the last in our society (15:11-32). Although the father was under no obligation to restore his profligate son to filial status, a sense of compassion and justice still compelled him to do just that. Like the prophets who excoriated the religious leaders of their day for their empty rituals, Jesus emphasized that the hope of God's kingdom belonged not to the scribes and Pharisees—outwardly pious, yet inwardly callous and corrupt—but to the poor.

If we want to see Jesus' own blueprint for justice, his own manifesto for social witness, we need only look at the text of his first sermon, preached in the synagogue at Nazareth (Luke 4:14-20). It is significant that the sermon follows immediately on the heels of Jesus' temptation in the wilderness (Luke 4:1-13). "Full of the Holy Spirit," Jesus is first tempted by the devil to use his divine power to maintain himself in comfort by commanding a stone to become bread. In the second temptation, the devil offers Jesus "all authority and glory" over the kingdoms of the world if only he will worship him. Finally, Jesus is tempted to use his divine power to advertise his mission and prove his divinity by subjecting himself to danger, in the sure knowledge that no harm would befall him. He rejects all these alternatives and chooses instead the way of the cross.

Immediately after these temptations and still gripped by the Spirit, Jesus goes on a preaching mission in Galilee, the region in which he grew up. The last stop is his hometown, Nazareth. By choosing as his text a prophecy by Isaiah, he makes it clear to his hearers that the power of the Spirit would be used for a very different purpose than his own aggrandizement and glorification. Instead, Jesus quotes Isaiah and proclaims:

> The Spirit of the Lord is upon me,
>> because he has anointed me
>> to bring good news to the poor.
> He has sent me to proclaim
>> release to the captives
>> and recovery of sight to the blind,
> to let the oppressed go free,
> to proclaim the year of the Lord's favor.
>
> (Luke 4:18-19)

These words speak of the Messiah's ministry to people in distress, and Jesus announces that they are prophecies of his own coming. The people in the synagogue, however, were amazed that "Joseph's son," someone whom they knew, could make such an utterance. It is interesting to note that they reacted with astonishment, not admiration or appreciation. They marveled at what he had to say, but they did not take it to heart. In fact, that astonishment turned to anger, for we read next that they ran Jesus out of town and attempted to throw him off a cliff! Perhaps this should serve as a warning to today's prophetic preachers. In his preaching Jesus had made it clear that this ministry was not to be a chaplaincy to the chosen band of believers, but was to be one that embodied a commitment to the dregs—the flotsam and jetsam—of society. In choosing the passage from Isaiah, therefore,

Jesus emphasized that his ministry would be dedicated to upholding justice.

This passage is helpful on many levels. First, it emphasizes the fact that a ministry of justice and social witness is absolutely central to our faith. In the "inaugural address" of his public ministry, Jesus proclaims that what we have become fond of calling "outreach" is a priority of his ministry. Second, the passage suggests that social witness for the Christian carries with it an inherent risk. Jesus was rejected at Nazareth, and he continued to meet with opposition from members of the "establishment" throughout his earthly ministry. This scenario has often played itself out in the Episcopal Church on occasions when the church has moved from a model of chaplaincy to one of advocacy—that is, when it leaves the comfort of its own community and ventures out to minister to "strangers and aliens." Although Jesus makes it clear that such actions are at the *heart* of what it means to be the church, the church's advocacy on behalf of the marginalized has often been rejected on the contention that such activities are not the church's business!

∼   **The Church and Human Rights**
The baptismal covenant in *The Book of Common Prayer* incorporates these biblical themes and spells out our mandate to social witness. Part of our "marching orders" as newly baptized Christians is "to seek and serve Christ in all persons, loving our neighbor as ourselves," and "to strive for justice and peace among all people, and respect the dignity of every human being" (BCP 304-5). These expressions are not just catchphrases. Understanding them is at the very core of our work as Christians.

Remember, too, that Job asked, "If I have rejected the cause of my male and female slaves, when they brought a complaint against me; what then shall I do when God rises up? When he makes inquiry, what shall I answer him?" (31:13-14). Job suggests that, although some people have been endowed with worldly wealth and power, everyone is of equal value before God. For all Christians, and perhaps especially for Episcopalians (who, like all Anglicans, place great store in the Incarnation, in which God takes on human flesh and so makes everything holy), this concept of common humanity takes on special significance. We worship a Lord who assumed the form of a slave and was obedient to the point of death on the cross. Does not God want us to show the same love and compassion for others that has been shown to us? The concept we call "human rights" is basically grounded in our belief that God places value on each person. The recognition of one another's human rights is the cornerstone of justice, which in turn is grounded in love. We are, therefore, called upon as Christians to uphold and execute justice as an expression of the love that God holds for all of us.

While few Christians in general, or Episcopalians in particular, would quarrel with such a description of their Christian responsibility, there is not always agreement regarding those to whom it should be applied. In our society, for example, most would agree that all groups are entitled to their inalienable rights (to borrow a phrase from the Declaration of Independence), but some Americans may oppose legislation enacted to ensure that such rights are accorded to particular groups. The civil rights that all Americans have, such as access to employment and educational opportunities, are not normally questioned today, but whether an affirmative action policy should be in place to help guarantee those rights is now the subject of heated debate in this country.

Although the execution of justice and the carrying out of our social witness are biblically mandated, not all members of the church agree about how they should be accomplished. One reason for this disagreement is that people read the Bible with different sets of lenses. "The most common problem in using the Bible as a resource for ethics," Michael Johnston rightly observes, "is that we often come to its pages not for advice on who we ought to be but for endorsement of who we are. . . . In fact, we tend to make up our social values as we go along . . . and then we impose them on the pages of the Bible."[9]

Another factor is that the scriptures are not the only source that informs our thinking. In the Anglican tradition, for example, we claim allegiance to the so-called three-legged stool of scripture, tradition, and reason, a concept espoused by the Anglican divine Richard Hooker in his *Laws of Ecclesiastical Polity*. Thus, some church members hold the view that while women should be accorded rights in the same way as men, the *tradition* of a male priesthood precludes the possibility of the ordination of women to a sacerdotal office. Others, to cite a further example, drawing on both their interpretation of the Bible and of the church's traditional moral teachings, believe that persons of homosexual orientation are not entitled to the protection of the laws of the land or of the church.

Although the church is still wrestling with how the scriptures should guide us in response to particular issues, most Christians agree that we should look to the Bible to chart the course of our social witness. In a hymn about the Bible, James Quinn speaks to its ability to inspire us to be the body of Christ and to witness in Christ's name. Motivated by compassion and a zeal for justice, we find in Holy Scripture the power to remove impediments that prevent us from being of service to others:

> Word that caused blind eyes to see,
> speak and heal our mortal blindness;
> deaf we are: our healer be;
> loose our tongues to tell your kindness.
> Be our Word in pity spoken;
> heal the world, by our sin broken.[10]

Chapter Two

The Church of England

> *Christianity is far more a polity than a system. . . . Christ came to establish a kingdom, not to proclaim a set of opinions. Every man entering this kingdom becomes interested in all its relations, members, circumstances; he cannot separate himself in any wise from them. . . . In this highest sense, the churchman must be a politician. . . . If he is a citizen of the world, he is also a citizen of his own country, and everything which affects its weal or woe, everything which concerns the bodily or the external, as well as the spiritual condition of its inhabitants, must be important to him.*
>
> —F. D. Maurice,
> The Kingdom of Christ

Outreach is a subject that has received much attention in the Episcopal Church in the last few decades. Parishes—large and small, urban, suburban and rural—increasingly demonstrate a commitment to address the needs of the communities in which they find themselves. As vestries prepare parish budgets, they often strive to ensure that a certain portion of their income is used for mission, and not just maintenance—that money is spent beyond the walls of the parish and not just within them. Churches are flinging open their doors to house soup kitchens, food and clothing pantries, shelters for the homeless and abused, and self-help groups such as Alcoholics Anonymous.

This sense of commitment is reflected in the liturgies of our prayer book. We not only pray "for the victims of hunger, fear, injustice, and oppression" and for "the sick, the friendless, and the needy" (BCP 392), but in our intercessions we also pray that we will be empowered to do something to improve the lot of such persons. We hold up before God "the poor, the persecuted, the sick, and all who suffer...that they may be relieved and protected" (BCP 390). We ask that God will "comfort and heal all those who suffer in body, mind, or spirit," and we express the wish that God will "give them courage and hope in their troubles, and bring them the joy of [God's] salvation" (BCP 389). We beseech God to "have compassion on those who suffer from any grief or trouble; that they may be delivered from their distress" (BCP 387).

In other words, it is our hope that as the people of God, we may be agents of change in society, that as Christ's body we may be instruments of the transforming power of the gospel. Here our exemplar is Jesus himself, who consistently ministered to the *physical* as well as spiritual needs of people who sought him out. In his encounters with the paralytic, the epileptic, the man with a withered hand, the woman with a flow of blood, and others who found themselves afflicted, Jesus did not simply assure them that all would be well in the "sweet bye-and-bye," but instead healed their infirmities. When confronted by a hungry crowd, Jesus fed them before he preached to them. "The great miracle of the Incarnation," in the words of one Anglican preacher, "resulted in the redemption of the souls of men; but our Lord still had time to heal their leprosy, to enlighten their blindness, and to cure their deafness."[1]

The church's current emphasis on this aspect of our faith might give the impression that such activity is something new in Anglican circles. Nothing could be further from the truth. A commitment to social justice has always been a hallmark of Anglicanism, and "in all times and in all places" the church has reached out and ministered to those in need. It has done so, in fact, because of a theology predicated on a strong belief in the Incarnation. As theologian James E. Griffiss expresses it: "Broadly speaking, mission is part of our conviction that the church is called to witness to the Incarnate Christ in all the conditions of human existence, including politics and economics, war and peace, literature and the arts, and in the natural world we inhabit."[2] In addition to being characteristic of Anglican thought, this view is clearly one that we also have in common with the earliest Christians. "Understanding Jesus in terms of the Incarnation," writes another scholar, "seems to have been precisely the engine that drove the early church's social awareness. . . . The early Christians could tell whether they were truly entering into the mystery of Christ by how well they were managing to love one another."[3]

The Oxford Dictionary of the Christian Church points out that one of the implications of the doctrine of the Incarnation is the principle of immanence—that is, the essential relatedness between God and humanity and a consequent emphasis on the value of culture and civilization in the purposes of God.[4] The immanence or omnipresence of God in the universe bears special relevance to an understanding of social witness. It is precisely because of the divine presence in all aspects of creation that God is concerned with and seeks to redeem every creature.

Such a God is in contrast to one who is wholly transcendent and unknowable. Belief in an immanent God, therefore, virtually eradicates the dichotomy between "sacred" and "secular" and declares, in effect, that there is nothing—no person, no issue, no condition, no circumstance, no political situation—that does not have a claim on the redemptive work of the gospel. Jesus certainly lived out such a commitment, much to the consternation of the Pharisees, as he associated with women, the "unwashed" Samaritans, tax-collectors, prostitutes and the other outcasts of his society. It is because of this example that we are empowered "to go out and look for Jesus in the ragged, in the naked, in the oppressed and the sweated."[5]

Emphasis on the Incarnation also characterizes John's gospel, in which the prologue speaks of the Word becoming flesh and dwelling in the world (1:14). In this passage the doctrine of the Incarnation is summarized, not simply as a divine act, but also in terms of its effects on the people of God. The God who is incarnate in Jesus Christ is, therefore, a being who is at work in the world—not a remote deity, but a God who is close at hand and active in the lives of all humankind.[6]

A well-known hymn about the mission of the church speaks to this incarnational theme of God's initiative and our human response:

> Lord, you make the common holy: "This my
>   Body, this my blood."
> Let your priests, for earth's true glory,
>   daily lift life heavenward,

Asking that the world around us
    share your children's liberty;
With the Spirit's gifts empower us
    for the work of ministry.[7]

These words remind us that precisely because Jesus entered the world as God incarnate, nothing in our world is intrinsically evil and everything can be sanctified by Christ's presence. It is at God's behest that the ordinary, that which is common, is offered up and sanctified, that is, made holy through God's agency. This hymn declares that we, empowered by the Holy Spirit and responding to the gift of the Incarnation, are called to share that gift with everyone with whom we come into contact. As Christians we are duty-bound to do so, because membership in God's kingdom means that we are also members of the human society in which we find ourselves. In response to the Incarnation, we are called to mission, to a life of sharing, to forgiveness, and to servanthood.

Continuing the tradition of the Hebrew prophets who preached that ministry to the helpless and oppressed was a necessary complement to divine worship, the incarnational theology that typifies Anglicanism has long considered social justice to be an indispensable component of religious practice. Whenever the church has flagged in its zeal, there have been those, not unlike the prophets of old, who have prodded and challenged it. Richard Hooker, Anglicanism's founding theologian who defended its beliefs on intellectual and rational grounds, argued that the church is the *extension* of the Incarnation. In his *Laws of Ecclesiastical Polity*, Hooker emphasized that the visible church is formed by God from the crucified body of Christ. It is through the church, and more particularly through its sacramental worship, that Christians have a relationship to the incarnate Lord. The Incarnation, therefore, has made possible the relationship that exists between God and humankind.[8]

These principles, moreover, have a direct effect on Hooker's social views. In his sermon entitled "The Nature of Pride," Hooker proclaimed: "God hath created nothing simply for itself; but each thing in all things ... has such interest, that in the whole world nothing is found whereunto any thing created can say, 'I need thee not.'"[9] The church, to Hooker, is primarily an agency of restoration, that is, the means by which we as human beings, by the power of the Holy Spirit, realize our full potential. It is the process described in the words of the eucharistic prayer, "And here we offer and present unto thee, O Lord, our selves, our souls and bodies, to be a reasonable, holy, and living sacrifice" (BCP 336). The church, in other words, exists for the benefit of humankind, and when it fails to function in this capacity, it falls short of its mission. When the sacraments are not instruments of such restoration but merely ends in themselves, they become objects of superstition. Hooker's commitment to social witness is inherent in his theology, in which the life of the individual is only meaningful in relationship to the social order and in service to the community.[10]

～ The Evangelicals

A later group of Anglicans espoused views about community service that were similar to Hooker's, but they arrived at their ideas by a somewhat different theological route. The Evangelicals, who flourished in the Church of England during the eighteenth century and whose sensibilities were more closely identified with what has been called "the Protestant face of

Anglicanism," emphasized personal conversion and salvation through faith in the atoning death of Christ.[11] Their personal piety grew in part out of an attempt to bring what we would call today a "reality check" to religious life in England, which had reached a low ebb, owing to what many saw as the worldliness and slothful indifference of the clergy. The Evangelicals' religious earnestness and distinctive brand of piety often made them unpopular, and in 1768 six students associated with the movement were expelled from St. Edmund Hall, Oxford, for having "too much religion."[12] Believing that "faith without works is dead," the religious fervor of the Evangelicals also translated itself into missionary zeal and social reform. The Church Missionary Society, an agency of the Church of England that sent missionaries to virtually every outpost of the British Empire, was a direct outgrowth of the Evangelical movement.

The piety of the Evangelicals may well be summed up in a statement of John Wesley following his conversion experience in 1738. Wesley proclaimed that he wished "to promote as far as I am able *vital practical religion* and by the grace of God to beget, preserve, and increase the life of God in the souls of men."[13] A priest of the Church of England, Wesley gathered around him a coterie of devout, earnest, and scholarly Christians who were variously described as the "Holy Club," "Bible Moths," and "Methodists." This group championed the causes of various disenfranchised groups, including coal miners and foundry workers. Moreover, during a missionary journey to the American colonies in the 1730s, John Wesley and his brother Charles not only attempted to minister to Native Americans and to debtors who had been deported from England, but also made enemies by preaching against the slave trade. George Whitefield, who came under the influence of the Wesleys at Oxford, was also a striking preacher who is credited with having, arguably, the most lasting influence on the religious conscience of the English-speaking world in the eighteenth century.

Another notable group of Evangelicals was the so-called Clapham Sect, named for the parish near London where it was founded. Composed largely of wealthy bankers and merchants and under the leadership of layman William Wilberforce, the Clapham Sectarians are not remembered either for their theological views or for their pulpit oratory. Rather, they sought to raise the moral standards of the populace through the establishment of Sunday schools and through the creation of agencies such as the Society for Bettering the Conditions and Increasing the Comforts of the Poor. They were also principally responsible for the Church of England's early missions to India and Sierra Leone.

The Clapham Sect's most important contribution to English life, however, was its effort to abolish the slave trade in the British Empire. After undergoing a conversion experience, Wilberforce exercised a lay ministry in Parliament, where he became an outspoken opponent of slavery. He was encouraged in this enterprise by his mentor John Newton, the cleric, preacher, and hymn-writer (perhaps best known for his hymn "Amazing Grace") who had once been captain of a slave ship. Continuing the Wesleyan tradition of "practical religion," Wilberforce believed that holding other human beings in bondage was an egregious sin and a blight on the moral and religious character of the English people. His relentless campaign against the slave trade is instructive, for he addressed not only the intrinsic evil of slavery (predicated as it was on the treating of human beings as chattel and not as children of God) but also the injustice of building up the wealth of the empire with the sweat and toil of slaves. Wilberforce's efforts spanned many years, and they resulted in the ending of the slave trade in 1807 and in the abolition of slavery throughout the British Empire in 1833—the year of his death.

The Evangelicals placed less emphasis on the church as an institution and on incarnational themes than other Anglican thinkers who both preceded and followed them. Nevertheless, armed with a zeal for the gospel and with an unbending commitment to personal conversion, they strove mightily, and not without considerable success, to correct injustices and to uphold the dignity of all people.

∼ The Christian Socialists

The fervor of the Evangelicals and the "awakening" with which they are credited were still not sufficient to convert the entire Church of England. Nor did their commitment to the poor result in an elimination of economic deprivation. Rigid class stratification continued to be an inescapable part of English life, and owing in part to the attitudes of the clergy toward the social classes, the church was simply not equipped to bring about radical social change. As one writer describes the situation, "Working-class men and women were not irreligious, though middle-class churchmen did not usually appreciate this, not having adequate tests by which to identify the nature of working-class religiosity."[14]

While such attitudes certainly existed, they by no means represented the whole picture, as there arose during the same period a veritable army of dedicated men and women committed to upholding the historic Anglican principles of social witness. Perhaps the most renowned was Frederick Denison Maurice, who has been called not only the greatest Anglican thinker of the nineteenth century, but also a prophet (although like most prophets, he was not fully appreciated in his own day). Owing to his exposure to a variety of views during his long and often torturous theological pilgrimage, he often challenged prevailing religious attitudes because he was acutely aware of the unbelief that usually lay hidden beneath conventional religion and popular orthodoxies.[15]

The son of a Unitarian minister, Maurice matriculated in 1823 at Cambridge University, which, as a Church of England institution, demanded that its students profess allegiance to the Articles of Religion. Because Maurice refused to do so, he was admitted as a nonconformist, that is, one who refused to conform to the doctrine of the established church. After a serious discernment process, however, he embraced Anglicanism, was baptized, and decided to seek holy orders. His theology, with its foundation in the Incarnation, espoused the belief that Christ is the head of the entire human race, and not just of the church. In teachings reminiscent of Hooker's emphasis on fellowship and community, he held that Christ's example demonstrates that neighborliness rather than individualism is the virtue for which all persons should strive. Moreover, Maurice insisted that the gospel must be heard in terms of its *universal* message. Indeed, it was this commitment to universality that later caused him to be relieved of his chair in theology at the University of London, when he acknowledged that he believed in universal salvation.

Maurice's theology also focused on the mission of the church in society and on the application of Christian principles to social reform. He argued that the church, as an agent uniquely suited for the spread of the gospel, ought to function as the conscience to the nation. In his *Theological Essays* (1853), he stressed that the world is the church without God, while the church is the world restored to its proper relationship with God. Maurice believed social injustices and evils to be irrational, the result of ignorance of God's divine order. The sacraments, too, figured prominently in his thought. They were seen as the means by which the union between Christ and the members of his kingdom was asserted and realized. And in an effort to transcend the barriers of class on which English society was predicated, Maurice launched "associations" composed of people from a variety of socioeconomic strata. These groups were founded on the belief that, since the kingdom of God encompasses the whole of creation, it is impossible for religion to be indifferent to any portion of the world in which God's creatures live, move, breathe, and have their being. As a result, Maurice's associations had as their purpose both the uplifting of their members and the dissemination of the principles he espoused.

The church, to Maurice, was made up of the family of humankind, and the sacraments were the means by which membership in that family was determined. This was symbolized most vividly in the sacrament of baptism, which Maurice envisioned as the mark of our universal fellowship in Christ. Baptism was not merely an event, but a rite that initiated "constant union" with God. It was the means whereby God enacted a covenant with each baptismal candidate, who was then adopted into Christ's body, the church. The sacrament of confirmation, furthermore, carried out and fulfilled the intention of baptism, for in confirmation the Christian acknowledged and acted on the duties and responsibilities inherent in church membership.[16]

If baptism initiated union between God and humankind, calling them into Christian service, then the Holy Eucharist, Maurice believed, ensured the continuation of that relationship. Through it, God communicated and ensured the preservation of the new life in Christ conferred through baptism. The three great ideas inherent in the eucharist were communion, sacrifice, and fellowship. Holy Communion was the common meal by which all Christians were fed, and the nourishment thus received enabled them to do service. The eucharist was, he wrote, "a Christianity of acts, not words, a Christianity of power and life, a divine, human, Catholic Christianity for men of all countries and periods, all tastes and endowments, all temperaments and necessities." In it, "the Lord of this society has bound himself to its members and they to him and to each other."[17]

Maurice and his colleagues Charles Kingsley and John Ludlow became known as Christian Socialists because they wished, it was said, to Christianize the socialists and to socialize Christianity. They believed the caste system on which Victorian England was established was incompatible with the teachings of the gospel, and they saw themselves as bridge-builders and mediators among the upper, middle, and working classes. The Christian Socialists were committed to the idea that the application of Christian principles would bring about improvement in all social relationships. Their theology might well be summed up in the words of Tennyson's In Memoriam: "Ring out, the feud of rich and poor, Ring in redress to all mankind."

Christian Socialism was foremost a social reform movement. It attacked the abysmal living and working conditions of the poor, and it pointed in horror to their lack of social mobility, their powerlessness, and the injustices of the court system. The Christian

Socialists were unrelenting in their criticism of the established Church of England, which had been all but impervious to the plight of the working classes. Kingsley, ordained in 1842, sought to effect the betterment and uplifting of the lower classes through education and what he called the "cooperative principle." Ludlow, a lawyer, was probably the most intellectual of the trio and clearly the most radical, for he had spent time in France at the time of the French Revolution. Expanding on Maurice's thought, he maintained that injustices were the products of a social and economic system that isolated and disenfranchised the poor. He suggested that the system itself needed to be thoroughly transformed—spiritually, morally, and intellectually. The Christian Socialists also engaged in practical relief work, founding workshops for tailoring, building, and other crafts. Maurice himself established both the Working Men's College (the first institution of higher education for men not from the upper and middle classes) and the Queen's College for Ladies (the first serious enterprise for the higher education of women in Britain).

The Christian Socialist movement seemed, on its face, to be a failure: the hierarchy of the church remained indifferent to the thought that they should minister to the poor, and those for whom the movement was intended were generally unresponsive. Yet it nonetheless marked the revival of a social consciousness within the Church of England. Through an incarnational and biblically-based theology, Maurice and his companions introduced Victorian Anglicans to the idea that the suffering of the masses and the lopsided distribution of wealth responsible for it were contrary to God's plan. They emphasized, moreover, that it was the church's duty to be a champion of the oppressed, not a chaplaincy to the status quo. Inspired by this example, subsequent reform groups in the church (such as the Christian Social Union and the radical Christian Socialist League) carried on the struggle that Maurice and others had begun.[18]

～ The Tractarians and Anglo-Catholics

Another group with entirely different theological emphases also emerged in nineteenth-century England and stressed the importance of social ministries. Called the Tractarians because they published theological treatises collectively entitled *Tracts for the Times*, this group initially placed a strong emphasis on the doctrine of apostolic succession, on the prayer book as a rule of faith, and on the divine origins of the Church of England. They believed that the roots of Anglicanism were traceable not to the Reformation of the sixteenth century but to the earliest days of Christianity. As a result, they saw the ancient church as a source of sanctification and as a model for contemporary Christianity. Strongly incarnational like the Christian Socialists, the Tractarians appealed to the early church fathers, whom they idealized as transformers of the world. In addition, a later generation of Anglo-Catholic parish priests, inspired by Tractarianism, ministered to the poor out of a belief that the church was *catholic* (from the Greek word meaning "universal") and therefore was duty-bound to be inclusive.

Although Anglo-Catholics are best remembered (and often maligned) for introducing the "smells and bells" of ritualism into church life, their alleged preoccupation with the externals of worship represents only one aspect of the impact they made. Because of their assertion that the Church of England was part of ancient, catholic Christendom, the Tractarians entreated Anglicans to embrace theological teachings of an earlier era, antedating the classism, elitism, and racism that infected the English church and distorted the gospel message it tried to preach. To the Tractarians, the church, far from catering to the elite, should demonstrate a bias for the poor.

Three priests and scholars from Oxford were in the forefront of the catholic revival that came to be known as the Oxford Movement. John Henry Newman, an Anglican vicar of St. Mary's, Oxford who later converted to Roman Catholicism, was unquestionably the leading spirit of this movement. His sermons, based on a systematic study of the early church fathers, had a profound effect on the spirituality and social conscience of the entire nation. Developing the idea of the *via media* first addressed in the writings of Hooker, Newman maintained that the Church of England had upheld the patristic tradition and thus occupied an intermediate position between Roman Catholicism and Protestantism. In a tract entitled "Adherence to the Apostolical Succession the Safest Course," John Keble, an Anglican priest, professor of poetry at Oxford University, and close friend of Newman, urged Anglican clergy to take a high view of their privileges and duties, including a reexamination of the assumption that they should minister primarily to the upper classes. And Edward Bouverie Pusey, Regius Professor of Hebrew at the University of Oxford, was a passionate preacher who did much to reintroduce an understanding of the role of the sacraments in the life of the Church of England. Indeed, he believed the sacraments to be their most efficacious when, as evidence of the Incarnation, they were used to strengthen the lot of the poor:

> If we would see Him in his Sacraments, we must see him also, wherever He has declared himself

to be, especially in His poor. Real love, to Christ, must issue in love to all who are Christ's, and real love to Christ's poor must issue in self-denying acts of love towards them. . . . The poor, rich in faith, have been the converters of the world; and we, if we are wise, must seek to be like them, to empty ourselves of . . . our abundance [and] self-love, even as He emptied Himself of the glory which He had with the Father, . . . and made Himself poor to make us rich.[19]

Another important aspect of the Anglo-Catholic movement was the founding of religious orders, in which the vows of poverty, chastity, and obedience became outward and visible signs of the renunciation of wealth and privilege by many who joined them. For example, the Community of the Resurrection (known as the Mirfield Fathers) was organized specifically to work among the poor, both at home and abroad. This order had a profound effect on Archbishop Desmond Tutu, who was moved by the willingness of Trevor Huddleston, a Mirfield Father in South Africa, to violate conventional race relations by tipping his hat to Tutu's mother. Later archbishop of the church in South Africa, Huddleston was a staunch opponent of apartheid and did much to shape Tutu's own spirituality, theology, and ethics.[20] Herbert Kelly founded the Society of the Sacred Mission for the purpose of ministering to boys from poor families, while the renowned hymn-writer John Mason Neale founded the Sisterhood of St. Margaret in order to educate girls (itself a radical innovation) and to care for the sick. Its American province of the Sisterhood of St. Margaret has for more than fifty years operated hospitals and orphanages in Haiti.

In an age in which worship in the Church of England was typically restrained, earning the church the epithet of "the Tory party at prayer," Anglo-Catholicism was in many ways countercultural, based on a sacramental emphasis on outward and visible signs. They literally took their religion into the streets. Clergy in richly adorned vestments, acolytes and choristers in attendance, could be seen celebrating religious festivals in the streets of London and other urban areas where their parishes were located. This liturgical extravagance stood in striking contrast to the underprivileged neighborhoods where the churches often were found, but rather than offending the poor, it gave them a taste, as it were, of the heavenly Jerusalem. The Tractarians' understanding of the Incarnation also meant that all the senses should be brought into play in worship—eyes beholding magnificently appointed churches; ears hearing glorious music and hymnody; nostrils smelling the redolent fragrances of incense; and tongues tasting the bread and wine that had become Christ's body and blood. The members of religious orders stood out as countercultural in a different way. The dour habits and abstemious customs of monks and nuns were emblematic of the vows by which they renounced the standards and mores of their society.

～ Archbishop William Temple

While the Anglo-Catholics were often flamboyant ritualists who had the temerity to challenge the church establishment, William Temple was the embodiment of the church establishment. His father Frederick had served as bishop of Exeter and bishop of London before becoming archbishop of Canterbury when William was sixteen years old. Throughout his ministry, William Temple spoke from positions of power and prestige within the church, and he served as arch-bishop of York (1929–1942) and Canterbury (1942 until his death in 1944). Thus, when he wrote in *Christianity and Social Order* that the Church of England had abandoned all concern for social justice, he could not be dismissed as an iconoclastic malcon-tent or idealistic dreamer. His words, written in a book whose purpose was to make the church's voice heard in matters of politics and economics, was a profound indictment of the failures of the institution he had been called to lead.

Among the factors that influenced Temple's com-mitment to social witness was the period he spent as bishop of Manchester, a city located in the industrial heartland of England. When a general strike of coal workers took place, Temple maintained that it was the church's *duty* to mediate between conflicting parties. While in Manchester he also chaired the group that planned the Conference on Politics, Economics, and Citizenship, which sought to discern the will and pur-pose of God in political, social, and industrial life. It is no coincidence, then, that Temple published *Christus Veritas*, which contains his most significant writings on the Incarnation, during his time in Manchester. He saw the Incarnation as the foundation stone of the faith and the church as the extension of that divine act, drawing people and nations into the fellowship of the Holy Spirit and completing the transforming work of Christ in the world.

In applying these principles to specific circum-stances, Temple believed that the church, as an advo-cate on behalf of those who suffer, is justified in challenging the existing social system in the name of justice. Although Temple espoused what might be called a high doctrine of the ordained ministry and the role of the episcopate, he was, nevertheless, one of the first to articulate the duties of the laity in carrying out the church's goals. In *Christianity and Social Order* he cited the example of William Wilberforce in ending the slave trade and noted that "nine-tenths of the work of the Church in the world is done by Christian people fulfilling responsibilities and performing tasks which in themselves are not part of the official system of the Church at all."[21] Thus, the most important work of the church was to make good Christian men and women who manifest the Spirit of Christ in their personal, family, and social relationships.

Like William Laud, his seventeenth-century predecessor as archbishop of Canterbury, Temple saw himself as a friend of the poor with a genuine compassion for justice. As he wrote in *Citizen and Churchman*, the vocation of the Christian "is to dedicate himself in the power of love to the establishment of justice."[22] He thought the church's mission, especially toward the disadvantaged, was severely diminished by those who envisioned Christian duty only in terms of love, and not in terms of concrete justice. In Temple's theology, love is the predominant principle, but justice is its primary form and expression. He lambasted the ineffectiveness of those who did not translate their philosophy into action, and he maintained that Christians must *work* for justice, thereby fulfilling their responsibilities to God and fellow citizens alike. Consecrated bishop soon after the end of World War I and dying while World War II was raging in Europe, Temple had to address a rapidly changing world that previous centuries of Anglicans could never have envisioned. In this context, he synthesized traditional Anglican teachings with social witness and brilliantly applied theological principles to the exigencies of time and place.

Since the time of the Reformation, Anglican thinkers, like the Hebrew prophets, have interpreted the signs of the times for their people. The Christian Socialists and the Tractarians, for example, all envisioned the church as an agent of transformation, capable of effecting change in social structures through a ministry of word and sacrament. Because an incarnational faith holds that God takes the initiative in moving toward us, and because Anglicans believe that Christ has "raised our human nature on the clouds to God's right hand" (as a hymn reminds us[23]), we have a clear mandate that the church, as Christ's body, must be instrumental in inaugurating God's kingdom on earth. Seen in this light, the question asked of us in the baptismal covenant—"Will you strive for justice and peace among all people, and respect the dignity of every human being?" (BCP 305)—also takes on new meaning. We know that this entails far more than simply volunteering in a soup kitchen or an after-school program. Our grounding in an incarnational understanding of the universe, which is the great legacy bequeathed by four centuries of Anglican thought, enables us to comprehend that our social witness—striving for justice in the name of Christ—is an integral part of our Christian lives. In this light we answer resoundingly in the baptismal covenant: "I will, with God's help."

Chapter Three

The Episcopal Church

The church does not exist for itself alone, or chiefly, but for the world around it. Its mission is to the world, and if it does not gain the world, its mission fails of its great end.

—James Coulton,
The Genius and Mission of the Protestant
Episcopal Church in the United States

Thanks to the victory of the colonial forces in the American Revolution, the Episcopal Church came into being. No longer an overseas outpost of the diocese of London, the fledgling American branch of Anglicanism began, at the end of the eighteenth century, to carve out its own ecclesiastical identity. The English prayer book was modified to suit the needs of a people who were citizens of a republic and no longer subjects of a king. The consecration of Samuel Seabury in 1784 meant that the church that had chosen to call itself "Episcopal" would, appropriately enough, have its own *episkopoi* ("bishops," literally, "overseers"). Although no distinguishable "American" theology emerged for at least the first hundred years of the Episcopal Church's existence, the heritage of Puritanism as well as the feisty, independent spirit of the former colonists meant that the polity of the new church would be both more congregational and more decentralized than that of the Church of England.

As ethicist Robert Hood observed in his book, *Social Teachings in the Episcopal Church*, it was in the area of social witness that the mother church had the most identifiable influence on her American daughter, for many Episcopalians in the mid- and late .nineteenth century adopted and espoused the ideas of the Christian Socialists and the Tractarians. However, the social teachings of the Church of England made the greatest impact neither on the seminaries nor on the formal theology and church policies, but on individuals, both clerical and lay.[1] Some of them were voices crying in the wilderness; others were visionaries; still others exercised nothing less than prophetic ministries. And like the Old Testament prophets, they were often silenced, dismissed, ignored, or ostracized. Even a cursory study of church history shows that decades and even centuries may pass between the first notice of a social injustice and the church's *official* response to redress it. This is because the church, like other institutions, tends to be conservative, rigid, and by nature resistant to change. As a result of this conservative bent, much of what the church has done officially has resulted from outside pressures, the church reacting to a situation rather than initiating an action.[2] An old parody of the hymn "Onward, Christian soldiers" is not far from the mark: "Like a mighty tortoise moves the church of God. Brothers, we are treading where we've always trod."

Despite this somewhat bleak picture, social witness in the Episcopal Church has been the story of those who have stepped forward and bravely encouraged the "tortoise" to emerge from its shell and explore unfamiliar terrain. We shall see how this phenomenon—

initial inaction on an official level followed by prodding from individuals and the development of new
theological positions on social issues—manifested
itself especially during the Civil War era (in the controversy over slavery) and at the time of the civil
rights movement (in the struggle over racial equality).

∽ **Slavery and the Civil War**
The American political landscape underwent unprecedented upheaval before, during, and after the Civil
War, when fundamental issues of race, economics, and
social order were in the balance. Because of those
issues, and more significantly, because the Civil War
was fought largely over the institution of slavery,
churches were embroiled in the sectional controversy
whether they wished to be or not. Leading figures
within most mainline Protestant denominations condemned slavery outright, and as a result the
Presbyterian, Methodist, and Baptist churches—their
northern and southern branches espousing diametri-
cally opposing views—all split over the issue in the
1830s and 1840s. By contrast, the Episcopal Church
never formally condemned slavery. While economic
self-interest and deference to southern slaveholders
were certainly factors, the Anglican penchant for
compromise, personal ties between northern and
southern clergy, and the fact that many Episcopalians
convinced themselves that slavery was merely a political matter outside the church's purview helped keep
the denomination united. Since the church clearly
abhorred ecclesiastical schism more than the suffering
of people held in bondage, it is questionable (as
African American bishop John Burgess commented in
1962) "whether in the long run unity was worth the
price of moral indecision."[3]

Although no organic separation ultimately took place, Episcopalians residing in the eleven states that seceded from the Union found themselves in an untenable position and, as a consequence, were forced to form a separate body—the Protestant Episcopal Church in the Confederate States of America. The position of the new, if short-lived, denomination was unambiguous: it not only defended the existence of slavery but also maintained that slavery was part of the divine plan. The 1862 pastoral letter of the Confederate House of Bishops reminded masters of "their obligation, as Christian men, so to arrange this institution as not to necessitate the violation of those sacred relations which God has created, and which man cannot, consistently with Christianity, annul."[4] Since Episcopalians in the north never officially recognized the existence of the Confederate body, however, the secessionist church was able quietly to reunite with the church in the United States at the end of the war. By the time of the 1868 General Convention, in fact, all dioceses were once again present and accounted for at the national gathering. The fact that the presiding bishop, John Henry Hopkins of Vermont, had been a proslavery advocate and Confederate sympathizer was of immeasurable benefit in the virtually seamless process of ecclesiastical reconciliation after the Civil War.

Yet despite the unwillingness of the General Convention to condemn slavery itself, several individual Episcopalians did so in no uncertain terms. Some laymen, such as William Jay and John Jay (descendants of revolutionary-era statesman John Jay), were outspoken abolitionists. And among the clergy, Alexander Crummell (an African American missionary in Liberia) and Phillips Brooks (then rector of Holy Trinity Church in Philadelphia) wrote tracts supporting abolition and published statements encouraging the church's support of the Union. These voices were to have a decided effect on the actions of the General Convention of 1862, when the church officially censured secession and the Confederate military cause.

With the carnage of the battle of Antietam and Lincoln's Emancipation Proclamation fresh in the minds of church members, the Civil War created a crisis situation that compelled even the normally non-confrontational Episcopal Church to take a stand. In a pastoral letter invoking Romans 13:1 ("Let every person be subject to the governing authorities; for there is no authority except from God") and drawing on language in the Great Litany of the prayer book that condemned acts of rebellion, the House of Bishops rebuked the Confederate leadership for engaging in sedition and so resisting the biblical mandate to obey the lawful authority of the United States government.

As we attempt to trace the development of a theology of social witness on the part of the Episcopal Church, this pastoral letter is of pivotal importance. Robert Hood, who describes this letter as the "first instance of a social teaching" on the part of the Episcopal Church, says that its reasoning exhibits "four pillars" of thought. First, the text emerges from and addresses a particular context or situation; that is, it theologizes in response to a specific condition in society rather than simply promulgating "generic" social truths. Second, it appeals to Holy Scripture as the norm and point of reference. Third, it cites the teachings of the prayer book. And fourth, it presents a "church-type" understanding of the relationship between the denomination and American government—a recognition that the Episcopal Church ought to be the guardian of the public morality of its nation.[5] In other words, this letter signaled the initial effort on the part of the Episcopal Church to envision itself as other than a chaplaincy to special-interest groups within its own constituency (in this case, the southern planter class). Instead, the bishops saw the church as an advocate for the interests of all its members and, by extension, for the whole society in which it lived.

This final point cannot be overemphasized. Like the American nation itself, the Episcopal Church underwent a sea change during and after the Civil War. The war had done far more than settle a political dispute; it had profoundly changed the conditions of American life and forced church leaders to face a new and unprecedented range of social questions. Paramount among these, owing to the manumission of several million slaves, was the reexamination of the church's ministry to blacks. Beginning with the establishment of the Protestant Episcopal Freedman's Commission in 1865, the church (in a spirit of what historian Gardiner Shattuck calls "racial paternalism") founded a series of agencies and institutions designed to work among African Americans in the south.[6]

Adjustment to the new status enjoyed by blacks was by no means the only change the church had to make. Thanks to the emergence of industrial capitalism, the economy of the United States expanded rapidly in the three decades following the Civil War. The development of natural resources, the rise of the railroad, and the mushrooming of industry brought unprecedented wealth to a handful of entrepreneurs, not a few of whom were Episcopalians. Often called "robber barons," this group generally amassed its wealth on the backs of an often overworked, underpaid, and mistreated workforce. As a result, the church turned to the expanding cities as a new mission field. In addition, the arrival of immigrants from southern and eastern Europe required a redoubling of its efforts in major cities such as New York and Chicago, where the Episcopal Church founded parishes that not only catered to working men and women but also offered services in languages other than English.

✎ The Social Gospel

One response to the industrialization and growth of urban areas in the late nineteenth century was a reform effort called the Social Gospel, which flourished during the period between the Civil War and World War I. It represented the application of Jesus' teachings to politics, economics, and all the institutions of modern society—an approach to Christianity, it can be argued, as old as Holy Scripture itself. Returning to the Old Testament prophets for inspiration, these reformers emphasized the responsibility of human beings to inaugurate the kingdom of God on earth.

Under the leadership of figures such as Baptist minister Walter Rauschenbusch, Congregationalist pastor Washington Gladden, and Episcopal layman and economist Richard Ely, the Social Gospel was inspired by three major principles: the "Fatherhood of God," the "Brotherhood of Man," and the imminence of God's kingdom. Advocates of the movement stressed that church and society, theology and science, and religion and culture were all complementary, and they believed that teaching from the pulpit should draw on the light offered by the social sciences.

The movement's standard bearers did not mean to suggest that the churches had been uninterested in social issues before. Prior to this period, however, social ministry was usually a matter of local initiative, not church-wide policy, and it was generally limited to parish charities on behalf of helpless individuals such as widows and orphans. Emphasis on the separation of church and state and on so-called personal religion simply reflected the individualism that was dominant in American religion until the middle of the nineteenth century. Moreover, the prevailing view that clergy should not engage in politics had generally kept the church leadership from committing itself to an overarching, hands-on approach to social witness.

The appearance of a new brand of religious teaching, however, was signaled in the words of many of the hymns written at the height of the Social Gospel movement. Frank Mason North, founder and editor of *The Christian City*, wrote a hymn ("Where cross the crowded ways of life") in which he empathized with the plight of workers and expressed hope that the city would be redeemed by Christ:

> O Master, from the mountain side,
> make haste to heal these hearts of pain;
> among these restless throngs abide,
> O tread thy city's streets again.[7]

In the hymn "O holy city, seen of John," Walter Russell Bowie, rector of Grace Church in New York City, castigated the wealthy who had been indifferent to the poor in their midst:

> O shame to us who rest content
> while lust and greed for gain
> in street and shop and tenement
> wring gold from human pain,
> and bitter lips in blind despair cry,
> "Christ hath died in vain!"[8]

The Episcopal Church not only became strongly involved in the Social Gospel movement, but also was the first denomination to espouse improvement of the wages and living conditions of working men and women. In 1886 the House of Bishops issued a pastoral letter in which wealthy church members were reminded of their responsibility toward the poor. The bishops also argued that the church itself should be a mediator between the opposing forces of labor and capital. This position initially appeared so uncharacteristic of the Episcopal Church that the journal of another denomination was moved to wonder why "the Church of wealth, culture, and aristocratic lineage" was leading the way in social ministry.[9]

In fact, this emphasis, while surprising to some, was not at all new. The rise of both Anglo-Catholicism and Christian Socialism in England had certainly influenced Episcopalians in America, and the fact that the membership of the Episcopal Church was concentrated in cities, often living cheek-to-jowl with those who were victims of social injustices, added to the effect. Social control, benignly understood, was also a significant factor. Numerous scholars have emphasized how the Episcopal Church understood itself as a divinely-appointed agent of social unity. Indeed, as historian Henry May once quipped, Episcopalians never really lost touch with their roots in the English religious establishment and its "medieval dream of society guided and led by the church." Thus, in the minds of some leaders within the Episcopal Church, advocacy of the claims of workers represented an important step toward the prevention of anarchy and unrest in society as a whole.[10]

In the decade following the Civil War, various loosely formed groups began to discuss social problems afflicting the nation. By 1887, the Church Association for the Advancement of the Interests of Labor (CAIL) had come into being. Inspired by the incarnational theology of the English Christian

Socialists, this organization investigated the living and working conditions of laborers, offered mediation when strikes took place, and in general did much to bring the public's attention to the lot of workers in sweatshops and tenements. Not a few of the bishops who were active in this movement were, like many of the industrialists whose companies perpetuated the injustices, from old established families, and they were able to use their influence to convince socially prominent Episcopalians of the need for labor reform. Among those bishops were Henry Codman Potter of New York, who was personally involved in strike mediation; Charles Williams of Michigan, who inveighed against unfair practices in the nascent automobile industry; and Chauncey Brewster of Connecticut, an indefatigable advocate for the underprivileged. Priests active in the movement included William Rainsford, under whose leadership St. George's Church in New York became a center of the so-called institutional church movement (urban churches organized to provide not only worship but also a full range of social services); and James O. S. Huntington, founder of the Order of the Holy Cross, a monastic order for men that began as a ministry to poor immigrants on Manhattan's Lower East Side.

Even more influential than these clergy were the lay men and women of the Episcopal Church who were prominent in social reform activities. One of the leading Social Gospel figures was Richard Ely, professor of economics at Johns Hopkins University and the University of Wisconsin, who believed that "practical Christianity" provided the answer for most of his country's ills. Author of *The Social Aspects of Christianity* (1889), Ely argued that God called church members to work for the salvation of their society as well as of individual souls.

Frances Perkins had first been attracted to the Episcopal Church and the importance of social ministry while working at a Chicago settlement house in the early twentieth century. She served for several years in industrial relations positions for both the city and the state of New York, and in 1933 Franklin D. Roosevelt appointed her Secretary of Labor, the first woman ever appointed to a Cabinet position. In that capacity Perkins exercised considerable influence in the implementation of Roosevelt's New Deal programs, including the Social Security Act of 1935 and the Fair Labor Standards Act of 1938.

Vida Scudder, a professor at Wellesley College, was active as a prolific writer and dedicated reformer. In 1890 she joined the Society of Christian Socialists, and in 1911 she helped organize the Episcopal Church Socialist League. Scudder was also one of the leading forces in the Society of the Companions of the Holy Cross, a group of professional women, founded in 1884, who sought to reform both society and the church by integrating their spiritual lives into their outlook on social justice.

While the Companions of the Holy Cross were women who understood their apostolate to be in the world, many other women involved in social ministries in the Episcopal Church belonged to religious orders organized along the more traditional lines of vows of poverty, chastity, and obedience. Inspired by the Tractarians in England, they saw the religious life as the most effective avenue for their Christian service. Members of communities such as the Sisterhood of the Holy Nativity and the Community of St. John the Baptist dedicated themselves to working in orphanages, hospitals, shelters, and schools, almost always ministering to immigrants and others in impoverished areas. Engaged in similar ministries were the deaconesses of the Episcopal Church. The 1889 General Convention passed a canon that recognized the role of deaconesses in instructing candidates for baptism and confirmation and in caring for women and children. Required by church law to be either unmarried or widowed, these women were set apart to serve in parishes as Christian educators, administrators, and social workers.

∾ The Civil Rights Movement

Although the Episcopal Church and its social ministries suffered from the economic collapse of the Depression years, World War II helped spark a period of unprecedented religious growth throughout the United States. Still, the promise of the "American dream," embodied in the economic boom and religious revival of the early 1950s, was reserved almost exclusively for white Americans. Black veterans, returning from service in a segregated army, discovered that they could not enjoy the freedom at home they had helped to secure for the rest of the world. Life in the Episcopal Church after World War II sadly mirrored the realities of race in the rest of the country, and most black Episcopalians were obliged to participate in segregated parishes, schools, camps, and other institutions. Cognizant of these shortcomings, the church began, in some places, to take small steps toward redressing its most obvious racial flaws. For example, Bishop Payne Divinity School, founded for the theological education of African American clergy after the Civil War, was closed in 1949, and John Walker was admitted as the first black student at Virginia Theological Seminary in the fall of 1951. But it was not until the civil rights movement was in full swing that any systematic change began to take place within the Episcopal Church.

Two events are generally credited with starting the civil rights movement. The first, and more widely known, was the refusal of Rosa Parks, an African American seamstress, to give up her seat for a white passenger on a bus in Montgomery, Alabama, in December 1955. The second is the demonstration, in February 1960, at a Woolworth lunch counter in Greensboro, North Carolina, staged by African American students from North Carolina Agricultural and Technical College. Mrs. Parks's act of defiance led to the Montgomery bus boycott, spearheaded by a then little-known Baptist preacher from Montgomery, Martin Luther King, Jr. The students' action added "sit-in" to the lexicon of American history, and that tactic became "standard operating procedure" for protests against racially discriminatory practices in both the south and the north.

I can personally identify with this means of protest. In the summer of 1963, I participated in what was then touted as the first sit-in demonstration in the north. Singing one of the battle hymns of the movement, "Black and white together, we shall not be moved," scores of us sat down in front of cement trucks and other vehicles to impede progress at the construction site of the Downstate Medical Center in Brooklyn, New York. Mrs. Parks protested against segregated public transportation and the students in Greensboro demonstrated against segregated eating facilities, while the Brooklyn demonstrations focused on the fact that minorities were barred from the construction industry. What all of us had in common is that we were arrested and carted off to jail.

That local, grassroots initiatives such as Montgomery and Greensboro are seen as cradles of the civil rights movement is significant, for personal witness on the part of protesters (as well as the attention brought to their cause by their imprisonment, mistreatment, and even death) never failed to have an impact on the American public. Mrs. Parks later commented that she did not mean to start a movement but refused to give up her seat simply because she was tired. While she was probably, at a conscious level, referring to her fatigue after a long day's work, her words also imply that she was tired of the injustices that had been perpetrated against her and other African Americans. The civil rights movement ultimately prevailed because of this human dimension. At some point, most white Americans came to realize that blacks were merely asking for the same civil rights guaranteed by the Constitution that they had long taken for granted.

In the context of our discussion of Christian social witness, moreover, we must remember that the civil rights movement was first and foremost a religious movement. For example, all the civil rights rallies I attended in the 1960s took place in predominantly black churches. I was with black clergy from large Brooklyn congregations when I was arrested at the Downstate Medical Center, and once behind bars, we transformed our cells into chapels, as we prayed, read scripture, and burst into song. It was no coincidence that the black church served as midwife to the civil rights movement. It was uniquely suited for this role, for black congregations have provided not only spiritual nurture, but also social uplift and empowerment for its members throughout American history. The civil rights movement, therefore, was a natural extension of the ministry of the African American congregation in a segregated society. And at a deeper level, African Americans saw the civil rights movement as nothing short of a new Exodus. The identification with the Jewish people of the Old Testament, in bondage in Pharaoh's house and seeking liberation and refuge in a promised land, became the theological *leitmotif* of the movement.

The passionate response to the civil rights movement on the part of many in the Episcopal Church can be attributed to the fact that Episcopalians recognized racial prejudice as not merely a social problem but a sin and a matter of public morality. It is interesting to note, too, that Warner Traynham, an Episcopal priest and proponent of black theology in the early 1970s, challenged his denomination to be a liberator of the oppressed by emphasizing the traditional Anglican belief in the church as the extension of the Incarnation in society.[11] This is why some Episcopal leaders took bold and immediate steps to redress the blot on their church's image by participating in the 1963 March on Washington and in the Selma march of 1965. In this way, the Episcopal Church truly resonated to the words of Martin Luther King when he accepted the Nobel Peace Prize: "I refuse to accept the view that mankind is so tragically bound to the starless midnight of racism and war that the bright daybreak of peace and brotherhood can never become a reality."[12]

In the civil rights movement, as in the case of the Social Gospel movement, there was an army of people who, through their life and prophetic witness, challenged the church to be true to its moral and ethical ideals. Appealing to the biblical and incarnational themes that have characterized the Anglican approach to social witness, they spoke of their impatience with the church's tendency to be content with advocating just enough change to maintain social order while resisting full and complete transformation. As Bishop John Burgess commented about the continuation of racial inequalities in the Episcopal Church in 1967, "We can no longer depend upon gradualism. Tokenism tends to give the impression that all is well. All is not well and time has just about run out! We must have a crash program to correct the inequities that are the shame of our church.... Something must be done quickly."[13]

The Latin phrase *lex orandi, lex credendi* ("the law of praying is the law of belief") has usually been employed to describe the process through which new theological insights emerge in the life of the church. What this means is that many ideas and practices appear in the church's prayer life long before they move to the level of official teaching. They start at the grassroots before they receive an *imprimatur* from the church's hierarchy or power structure. I think such a paradigm can also be used to describe the evolution of social justice in the Episcopal Church. Advocacy on behalf of the working classes, commitment to a ministry with the urban poor, and opposition to racism were not ideas that originated in the House of Bishops or on the floor of General Convention. Rather, they began within the hearts and minds of individuals who did not wait for the institutional church to do something, but who recognized that, as members of the body of Christ, they truly *were* the church.

Despite being caricaturized as a self-serving denomination concerned mainly with ministering to the carriage trade, the Episcopal Church has in fact been a pioneer in the arena of social justice in the United States. While the official church has sometimes (and rightfully) been seen as slow to take action, when it has acted on behalf of social justice, it has often been the first religious body to do so. This was certainly true in connection both with the labor movement at the end of the nineteenth century and with the civil rights movement in the mid-twentieth century. Robert Hood's observation that "the Episcopal Church is quite untidy, undisciplined, unsystematic, and episodic when it deals theologically with social issues" is correct only insofar as it has never established a single set of guiding principles for Christian social witness.[14] Instead, the church's social teachings have developed organically in response to particular concerns and challenges. Prodded—sometimes gently and sometimes not so gently—by those who possessed, like Amos, the vision of a just society, the Episcopal Church has been shaped and molded into a body responsive to the demands of human need.

Chapter Four

Economic Justice

We live in a world in which it is not fashionable to speak of, or for, the poor. Political parties are embarrassed to speak of fairness, equity and justice for the poor. We live in a world where the human family has become increasingly divided—between the very few—those twenty percent who take for themselves eighty-three percent of the world's income, and the many who receive so little of the world's income. We live in a world in which money has more powerful rights than human rights. In a world governed and dominated by Mammon. Only amongst the faith communities does there seem to be any will to challenge Mammon. Only in our churches, our synagogues, our mosques and our temples does it seem possible to envision a different world and a different economy.

 —Njongonkulu Ndungane, Archbishop of Cape Town,
  "Remarks...to the Lambeth Conference Plenary
   on International Debt," *July 1998.*

It is impossible to consider the nature of economic justice without an assessment of the role of liberation theology, which interprets Christian faith from the experiences of suffering and struggle among the poor. As I mentioned in the first chapter in my discussion on God's "preferential option for the poor," liberation theology reads the Bible and the teachings of Christianity through the eyes of the oppressed. Since the lot of the poor is almost always a consequence of the disparities and injustices inherent in the distribution of the world's goods, it is no mere intellectual exercise. Part and parcel of such theology is a critique of society (of which the institutional church is an integral part) and the ideologies that sustain it. Although often identified with writers such as Gustavo Gutiérrez, Juan Luis Segundo, Leonardo Boff, and the martyred archbishop Oscar Romero, liberation theology is by no means unique to Latin America. Black theologians James Cone and Gayraud Wilmore, feminist theologians Elisabeth Schüssler Fiorenza and Mary Daly, the womanist theology (the black woman's corrective of feminist theology) of Kelly Brown Douglas and Delores Williams, and many of the theologies now emerging on the African continent are all examples of liberation theology.

While liberation theology has now gained a modicum of respect in academic and ecclesiastical circles, it was initially met with harsh criticism and rejection. A typical negative reaction was to say that theology (that is, talk about *God*) cannot emerge from or address the problems of a particular class of human beings. Instead, the opponents of liberation theology argued, "God-talk" is only valid when it is applicable to all of humanity. Such critics, however, made a number of false assumptions, and they forgot that Christian theology was once virtually the exclusive province of white, western European and North American males from privileged economic backgrounds. Liberation theology sought to provide a corrective to the prejudices inherent in writings formed by that social milieu, presenting an alternative intellectual outlook reflective of some very different life experiences. It should be noted, too, that several early liberation theologians were Roman Catholic clergy who were censured by the pope for criticizing the church structure and its teaching office, the *magisterium*. The papacy's response had an especially ironic twist, since several liberation theologians in Latin America were clearly inspired by documents about the church's attitude toward poverty that had first been promulgated by the Second Vatican Council.

Central to liberation theology is the notion of God's "preferential option for the poor." By this concept liberation theologians maintain that the scriptures contain a clear bias toward the oppressed. In the words of James Cone:

> The hermeneutical principle for an exegesis of the Scriptures is the revelation of God in Christ as the Liberator of the oppressed from social oppression and to political struggle, wherein the poor recognize that their fight against poverty and injustice is not only consistent with the gospel but *is* the gospel of Jesus Christ.[1]

Theologians such as Cone believe that those who fail to see this aspect of the gospel are not authentic Christians, and are guilty of upholding a deficient and anemic faith. Cone and others see the Bible not as a static entity, merely the repository of authoritative divine utterances, but as a living word that is daily encountered by the people. Indeed, according to Joerg Rieger, "the encounter with the underside of history" throws extraordinary new light on the biblical texts.[2] While it once was rare for the Bible to be in the hands of members of the Latin American underclass, many of them now read it precisely because they see it as having a freeing message for the oppressed. Liberationists envision the scriptures as being capable not only of transforming lives, but also (as Rieger suggests) of causing a radical redirection of the "social location" of Christian believers.[3]

For the liberation theologian, evidence of God's preferential option for the poor is found first in the story of the Exodus, the deliverance of slaves from bondage in Egypt. In the Exodus, God was disclosed as the liberator of the oppressed, and as a result the Exodus event became an archetype for the social ideas expressed in the preaching of the Hebrew prophets. In Amos, for instance, Yahweh says: "I brought you up out of the land of Egypt, and led you forty years in the wilderness, to possess the land of the Amorite" (2:10). Advocacy for the poor, Yahweh's cherished possession, also is a recurrent theme in Isaiah: "Seek justice, rescue the oppressed, defend the orphan, plead for the widow" (1:17). Psalm 72 speaks of God's blessings on the king who guarantees justice for the needy and helpless, while the book of Proverbs equates the giving of kindness to the poor with the honoring of God (14:31).

While the Old Testament provides a theological underpinning for the theory of the preferential option, it is in the New Testament that the liberation theologian sees this principle in action. According to James Cone, this aspect of the New Testament had traditionally been de-emphasized because, as "descendants of the advantaged class," most white biblical scholars were prone to "minimize Jesus' gospel of liberation for the poor by interpreting poverty as a spiritual condition unrelated to social and political phenomena."[4] Liberationists, on the other hand, call attention to the fact that the poor in Luke's Beatitudes (6:20) are not simply the "poor in spirit" mentioned in Matthew's gospel (5:3); they are in fact the oppressed and afflicted, the hungry and thirsty, the sick and captives who are unable to defend themselves against the powerful. Luke further emphasizes God's desire to liberate people from oppression when he describes the dreadful fate of the rich man who turned his back on the beggar Lazarus (16:19-30). But the element of liberation theology that is most disturbing to privileged Christians is the notion that the people whom they have marginalized will not merely be incorporated into the kingdom along with everyone else, but will in fact be the first into the kingdom. As Jesus tells the self-righteous Pharisees, "the tax collectors and the prostitutes are going into the kingdom of God ahead of you" (Matthew 21:31). The Jesus of liberation theology, moreover, is the literal embodiment of this concept. Christ's humanity is not an abstraction but, born in a stable and always in solidarity with those at the margins, Jesus incarnates the suffering humanity whom he comes to serve.

Liberation theology, taking its cue from both the Old and New Testaments, indicts those who oppress the poor or who are indifferent to their plight. As the gospels tell us, possessions and wealth are truly a hindrance to discipleship (Mark 10:17-25). Liberation theology calls the Christian community to take up the cause of the poor and to be a partner in solidarity with them as they struggle to liberate themselves from the shackles of economic injustice. As Gustavo Gutiérrez suggests, this represents "a new ecclesial consciousness and a redefinition of the task of the Church in the world."[5] By understanding the poor not as part of a hard-to-define spiritual plane but as flesh-and-blood inhabitants of "this fragile earth, our island home," liberationists challenge the church to be a tireless advocate for social change.

While starting from a very different premise than the liberation theologians, M. Douglas Meeks espouses a theology consonant with theirs. He argues that "because the church exists for the sake of God's love of the world," there can be no sound ecclesiology that does not consider the church's relationship to the world and its economy.[6] Meeks observes that not only is biblical language about God fundamentally economic, but economic language is also peculiarly theological, for concepts such as trust, fidelity, redemption, and debt are common to theological as well as to economic discourse. Seen in this light the Lord's Prayer, for example, takes on a deeper theological and political meaning—"forgive us our debts" no longer being simply spiritualized or privatized. Meeks further points out that, since the English word "economy" comes from two Greek terms, *oikos* ("household") and *nomos* ("law"), economy is the law (or governance) of the household. All justice, therefore, has to be economic in focus, for those who have been denied access to the *oikos* on account of race, gender, or age, for example, are also statistically more likely to be poor. Christians, he believes, should strive to ensure that all people find a place where, in the words of Ephesians, they are "no longer strangers and aliens, but . . . members of the household [*oikos*] of God" (2:19). The church must take seriously its character as the "household of God" by recognizing the pervasiveness of economic injustice and by working diligently to eliminate it.[7]

∿ The Lambeth Conference of 1998
The 1998 Lambeth Conference was particularly critical in regard to a Christian understanding of economic

justice. A large number of the bishops who assembled at this dicennial gathering of the world's Anglican bishops were, of course, from third-world countries. While their pronouncements on human sexuality received the most attention in the United States, the bishops also passed several significant resolutions that addressed the issues of economic justice and world debt. Influenced by the tenets of liberation theology, Peter Selby (bishop of Worcester) urged his colleagues not to fall into the trap of "business as usual," reverting to a time when it was axiomatic that the institutional church would identify with the privileged classes. "To place ourselves in solidarity with the debtors of the world, rather than with the so-called wisdom of its creditors," he said, "is a major test of our loyalty to Jesus Christ and our willingness as a communion of churches to live by what he teaches." The greatest burden confronting many nations, Selby emphasized, is the massive debt owed to the world's richest nations and financial institutions.[8]

To describe third-world debt as "massive" is almost an understatement, for the amount paid by debtor nations is in many cases more than ten times the amount initially borrowed. This debt seems even more extreme and unreasonable when we consider the fact that for centuries developed nations in Europe wrested both natural and human resources from developing countries, mostly in Africa. Now those industrialized countries, making no allowance for the fact that they achieved their wealth at the expense of the debtor nations, are lending money to their former colonies at exorbitant rates of interest. In this context, then, it is not surprising that developing nations are calling not just for the reduction of debt, but for its remission. According to a Lambeth communiqué, third-world countries were seeking "the cancellation of debt as a matter of justice, human dignity and equality." As Alfred Reid (bishop of Montego Bay in Jamaica) observed, "Debt relief is not enough. It leaves the system intact and it doesn't address its causes." Similarly, Archbishop Njongonkulu Ndungane of Cape Town pointed out that the effects of global poverty are not purely economic, but are also "about loss of dignity, being treated as nothing."[9]

The crisis of international debt, the bishops were quick to point out, is fundamentally a moral dilemma. As Peter Selby's remarks suggest, Anglican churches in industrialized countries can ill afford the luxury of doing what for so long has come naturally, namely, identifying with the power structures largely responsible for the present crisis. Instead, they must make a radical break and willingly identify with those for whom the system has proved oppressive. Since Selby and many of his fellow bishops at Lambeth envisioned solidarity with the poor as a gospel imperative, they cited the biblical concept of jubilee and called confidently for the release of "those who are captive to economic forces beyond their control, and liberty from their oppression by the chains of debt."[10]

~ **The Episcopal Church**

Looking at the history of the Episcopal Church over the past one hundred years, we have seen a discernible process of maturation in this denomination's approach to economic justice. During this period the church has moved from the mere expression of platitudes—simply urging workers and industrial giants in 1919, for instance, to practice "neighborliness, friendship and brotherhood" toward one another—to the adoption of more courageous and prophetic positions on the relationship of capital and labor.[11] Although General Convention was generally slow to speak out in forceful terms against the ills of society, individual church members—people like Richard Ely, Vida Scudder, and Frances Perkins—took up the banner of social reform in the church during the late nineteenth and early twentieth centuries. In the 1960s, however, the official leadership of the denomination finally began to give serious attention to economic justice.

John E. Hines, elected presiding bishop in 1964, should probably be given credit for enabling Episcopalians to address the issue of economic justice in a tangible and sustained way for the first time. Troubled by the racial and economic turmoil that plagued the nation's cities in the late 1960s, Hines challenged his church at the 1967 General Convention to stand beside and support those who were most oppressed and powerless in American society. His inspired vision was eventually realized in the creation of the General Convention Special Program (GCSP), which began operation in 1968 with a budget of several million dollars. Hines was also quick to identify the role that race and racism played in the arena of economic justice in the United States, and he saw the GCSP as an attempt on the church's part to atone for centuries of indifference to the plight of African Americans and the poor.

Despite Hines's optimism, the GCSP did not live up to the expectations of those who organized it. The program represented a radical departure from previous denominational ventures because it gave funds *directly* to community groups. Troubled by the Episcopal Church's long history of identification with the American power structure, the staff of the GCSP assumed that only radical groups outside (and sometimes even hostile to) the church could effect meaningful economic change. This attitude, however, encouraged those who worked for the GCSP to bypass diocesan bishops, parish rectors, and other church members—even the leadership of African American churches in ghetto neighborhoods—when making grants to the poor. The GCSP soon evoked such ire among most middle-class Episcopalians that protests forced the termination of the program after only six years of operation. Although John Allin (Hines's successor as presiding bishop) continued some of the aspects of the GCSP, he guaranteed that all future financial gifts by the denomination would take into account the needs and concerns of church members at the local level.

The Episcopal Church turned another major corner at the 1979 General Convention. Citing scriptural examples of God's never-failing commitment to outcasts, the convention declared that the church must necessarily continue Christ's ministry in the world. Episcopal parishes were called upon to forge coalitions with those adversely affected by a changing economy, working with disadvantaged people to find a solution to their plight. Doubtless inspired by this prophetic example, the Coalition of Urban Bishops in its Labor Day pastoral letter of 1979 declared that human labor is the way in which men and women participate in creation and in the building up of God's kingdom. The document also proclaimed that Christians should not tolerate any forms of inequality (racism, sexism, and economic exploitation) that impede the holy purposes of labor. This position represents a quantum leap from the bishops' pastoral letters earlier in the century, in which a spirit of cooperation and charitable forbearance between the rank-and-file and management was encouraged.

Inspired and empowered by these mandates, the 1982 General Convention pressed even further forward by adopting a resolution on "Jubilee Ministry."

This approach to economic justice was based on the year of jubilee described in the twenty-fifth chapter of Leviticus, when slaves in ancient Israel regained their freedom. The church's program, by analogy, was designed to empower those who had previously been powerless. The resolution also established the Office of Jubilee Ministry at the national church headquarters in order both to educate Episcopalians about poverty and to encourage them to take an active part in aiding the poor. Unlike the GCSP, this initiative was concerned as much with the education of rank-and-file Episcopalians as with the donating of money to the needy. In addition, the program presupposed that privileged church members would be forced to examine and confront the deleterious role they often played in the overall economy of the United States.

The contrast between this new approach—its philosophical underpinnings being reflective of the tenets of liberation theology—and the church's traditional posture toward the poor cannot be overemphasized. First, the concept of "joint discipleship" eschewed the long-standing notion that the church, like Lady Bountiful, dispenses largess, and it instead espoused the belief that a common humanity and commitment to Christ, not the economic disparity between donor and recipient, is the most critical factor for those working *with* the poor. Second, by challenging its membership to understand the facts of poverty and injustice, the church moved away from the perception of poverty as a pathology (which, in effect, blames the victim) toward an understanding of the forces at work in our society that cause economic privation and its attendant ills. Third, the church's jubilee resolution challenged Episcopalians to put their faith into action in order to foster the creation of a society characterized by economic parity.

In response to a proposal from the diocese of Michigan, the 1988 General Convention established the Ministry of Community Development and Economic Justice. Similar in concept to the GCSP, this program was intended to support local economic development projects, such as housing cooperatives, worker-owned businesses, and community-based credit unions. In endorsing this approach, the church took note of a changing economic landscape that was becoming increasingly more technological. Since jobs held by factory workers and those in the service industries were being eliminated, and since the communities dependent on such jobs were being adversely affected, Episcopal congregations were urged to stand in solidarity with those who had been displaced by the shifting economic tide. What distinguished this initiative from earlier programs like the GCSP, however, was the role that dioceses and parishes assumed as *investors*, not merely as grant-makers, in community organizations. Instead of providing stopgap measures for current programs, the approach adopted in 1988 helped ensure the long-term viability of local groups.

In the period since the 1960s, the church has also become aware of the fact that it can wield considerable financial influence as a shareholder in American corporations. A number of years ago, an Executive Council publication that examined the social policies of the Episcopal Church introduced the seemingly radical notion that the denomination ought to employ criteria other than the maximization of profits when formulating its investment strategy. Just as the church expects individual Christians to be responsible stewards of their money and possessions, the document said, so the denomination should employ its own economic power to frame a more just and equitable society. As a result of this new consciousness, a

committee on Social Criteria in Investments was
established as an arm of the Executive Council, and it
has functioned as a watchdog organization for the
church's financial portfolio for many years.

～ Implementing Economic Justice

In the various ways enumerated above, the Episcopal
Church at all levels now understands that economic
justice is central to its mission. Remembering the
mandate contained in the Bible, the church offers the
same "good news to the poor" that Jesus proclaimed
when he preached in the synagogue in Nazareth at the
beginning of his ministry (Luke 4:18-19). Having
spent more than a decade as part of the national
church structure, however, I know well the limita-
tions of this vision. Slick publications, catchy slogans,
clever acronyms, and sophisticated consultants in and
of themselves cannot ensure the success of every initiative. Recent church history is replete with examples
of programs that did not succeed because the people in
the "field" were less than enthusiastic about them and
refused to provide them with funding.

Economic injustices have been redressed only when
dioceses and congregations take it upon themselves to
use their resources to improve local conditions. There
are several examples of this phenomenon, among
them the Michigan Plan that the 1988 General
Convention adopted. The Michigan proposal provided
resources and assistance that enabled low-income
groups to develop their own land trusts, housing programs, businesses, and credit unions. More recently,
the diocese of Long Island, in partnership with Trinity
Church, Wall Street, and other ecumenical and inter-
faith partners, launched the Nehemiah Project, which
put the dream of home ownership within the reach of
low-income families.

If it is true, as three seasoned observers of church life have recently said, that "the vast majority of resources needed to carry out any ministry in our church is to be found at the congregational level," then this idea is especially applicable to the black urban parish.[12] Some reasons for this are obvious. Black parishes, whether their congregants are well-to-do or disadvantaged, are usually situated in what are now the nation's inner cities, and they have an understandable interest in community development. Other reasons that relate to the unique history of black congregations are not so obvious. Arnold Hamilton Maloney, a black priest who graduated from the General Theological Seminary in 1910, pointed out that whereas the "white church" exists so that its members may "pay God a call to offer their help in the difficult problem of guiding the course of the world," the black church, by contrast, is where "the problems of home and of the community are threshed out."[13] More recently, the authors of a definitive work on the African American religious experience have asserted that "the economic ethic of the Black Church was forged in the crucible of the slave quarters from whence an ethos...of survival and self-help emerged."[14] Having given life and sustenance to the civil rights movement, the black church has been concerned consistently with the liberation and empowerment of its people.

The Church the Messiah in Detroit and the Church of St. Edmund, King and Martyr in Chicago both exemplify this tradition of social involvement. In the late 1970s, a fire in a neighboring apartment building provided an important opportunity for ministry by the people of Messiah, Detroit. They responded with food, blankets, and clothing for the residents of the building who had lost most of their worldly goods. This spontaneous act of compassion opened the parishioners' eyes to the need for affordable housing, and as a result the parish bought the apartment building and renovated it, thus bringing the Messiah Housing Corporation into being. In a twenty-year period, the congregation and its housing corporation purchased and renovated half a dozen other properties, sponsored more than two hundred units of affordable housing, and repaired over six hundred family dwellings. A food pantry, food delivery service, and summer employment programs also emanated from this ministry. In reflecting on the fruits of his pastorate at Messiah (where he was rector for twenty-five years), Ronald Spann observed that creating affordable housing in communities of great need is not easy; it requires professional skill, patience, tolerance, and a profound understanding of human nature. Engagement in the public sector stimulated the inner strength of a congregation, he thought, and rooting out the causes of injustice and human suffering served as a form of evangelism by giving parishioners an opportunity to live the gospel.[15]

At a conference on Afro-Anglicanism held in South Africa in 1995, Richard Tolliver, rector of St. Edmund's, Chicago, presented a theological rationale for the economic justice programs of his parish. Tolliver serves as president of the St. Edmund's Redevelopment Corporation, which has now invested close to $20 million in the acquisition and renovation of multifamily apartment buildings in the impoverished neighborhood surrounding his parish. In his talk, he emphasized how his parish's role as a community developer is predicated on three key elements in the African American church tradition: first, the strong sense of cooperative economics fostered by West African culture; second, belief in the biblical calls for justice and righteousness; and third, the desire to uphold a religious system grounded in ministry to both the spiritual and the social needs of the community. Believing that "there can be no true economic development of the community until the spirit and the mind are free," Tolliver asserted that the work of his parish "does not begin with an analysis of community problems; it begins with the prophetic imperative, 'Let justice roll down like a mighty river, and righteousness like a never failing stream.'"

To Tolliver, the community is akin to a household (*oikos*), and for him there is no demarcation line between those who belong to his church and the people of the neighborhood. There are no "strangers and aliens," but all have an inherent right of access to the *oikos*. Tolliver also sees development as a theological concept that is concerned with perfection and sanctification—God's people moving toward realizing the "full stature of Christ." The parish's approach is a holistic one. Community economic development, when properly implemented, creates jobs and sponsors job training. It transforms programs like welfare that promote dependency and encourages low-income people to build new opportunities for themselves. It is about ministering to, with, and on behalf of those whom Jesus called "the least" of his brothers and sisters (Matthew 25:40).[16]

As Tolliver suggests, parish churches are often the last remaining stable institutions in communities that suffer from decay and blight. It stands to reason, then, that churches should take the lead in recreating the social fabric in the inner city. St. Edmund's has done its part by providing affordable housing, good education, and economic opportunity. St. Edmund's Academy, which had been closed prior to Tolliver's arrival in 1989, was reopened, and now it not only educates neighborhood children with love and sensitivity, but also enables those from the most disadvantaged families to attend a private school. The academy is an integral part of the parish's commitment to economic development through its "investment" in youngsters at the grade school level. The school provides the skills and the confidence needed to cope with the broader society, thereby helping to ensure that children will be able to break out of the spiral of poverty and emerge as productive citizens.[17]

It is imperative, for our own souls' health, that Episcopalians and other Christians continue faithfully to make progress in the area of economic justice. Indifference to the problems of the poor is not an option for us. As the Roman Catholic bishops in the United States reminded us in 1986, "Our faith calls us to measure this economy, not only by what it produces, but also by how it touches human life and whether it protects or undermines the dignity of the human person." They noted that "economic decisions have human consequences and moral content," and those decisions hurt as well as help people. The bishops challenged Christians to practice their faith in the world with "a spirituality that calls forth and supports lay initiative and witness not just in our churches but also in business, in the labor movement, in the professions, in education, and in public life." Finally, they asked the faithful to assume the role of advocates, "to speak for the voiceless, to defend the poor and the vulnerable, and to advance the common good."[18] These ideas have considerable value for the development of a theology of economic justice in the Episcopal Church, and we need to take them to heart.

One problem endemic to Episcopalians, however, is our inability in recent years to stick to a particular social strategy. We have become far more excited about short-term crusades than about long-term journeys or pilgrimages.[19] A glance at General Convention resolutions over the past two or three decades reveals that the church has flitted from one concern to another, a phenomenon that could well be described as "cause *du jour."* Prayer book revision, ecological awareness, women's ordination, sexism, and heterosexism have all vied with economic justice for attention. Moreover, because the Episcopal Church has long been identified with the privileged classes, its members have had particular trouble dealing with distinctions of race and class. In fact, the very invention of the concept of "multiculturalism," in which we purport to celebrate ethnic diversity, has grown out of an inherent discomfort with the idea that *racism* is still a major factor in everyday life. It is impossible, however, to address the problems of economic injustice without first recognizing the disadvantages from which people of color suffer in this country. Periods of introspection such as the one in which we now live usually bode ill for social witness in the church.

Despite this recent history, the church must be willing to go forward and learn from its past experiences. Although the GCSP, for example, was flawed because it ignored established constituencies within the denomination, its commitment to self-determination, dignity, and grassroots empowerment was certainly laudable. And while the Jubilee Ministry program did not accomplish all that it set out to do, we should not lose sight of its contributions in recognizing how local parish churches are the best agencies for carrying out our work in the arena of economic justice. At the present time, we must also see the relationship between local initiatives and the worldwide social problems identified at the 1998 Lambeth Conference. As Njongonkulu Ndungane reminded his fellow bishops, international debt is not just a matter for the poorest nations, but affects everyone everywhere. The archbishop's words about the social role of the church are telling and impressive. Since "we are perhaps the only global, national and local institution that will...fight for the poor," the church must always give a presence and a voice to the poor in its own life.[20]

Chapter Five

Race

The problem of racial and cultural relations is the number one social problem of our day. As such, it is the number one challenge before the Christian Church. And our Lord is judging His church, testing its loyalty to Him and its obedience to His word in terms of what it is doing to heal the divisions between men. . . . If, through God's grace, we rise to this challenge, future generations may look back on our day and declare, "it was then that the Christian Church began to live the Faith it proclaims."

—Joseph Pelham,
Department of Christian Social
Relations of the Diocese of Michigan, 1959

I cannot approach the question of race in the Episcopal Church dispassionately, nor do the editors of this series expect me to do so. I am an African American in my thirtieth year of ordained ministry, eleven years of which were spent as director of the Office of Black Ministries at the Episcopal Church's headquarters in New York. In that capacity, I was in charge of developing programs and special ministries for black Episcopalians. I strove to bring about a deeper understanding and mutual respect between blacks and whites, and by default as much as by design, I was the "official spokesman" for black issues.

One of the most enriching aspects of this experience was my collaboration with colleagues at the other "ethnic desks"—Native American, Asian American, and Hispanic. Having viewed the racial situation in the nation and in the church solely through the lens of the black experience, my work on the presiding bishop's staff served to broaden my appreciation of the struggles of other racial minorities. Traditionally marginalized in the life of the church, these ethnic groups together make up less than ten percent of all Episcopalians. Our job, in part, was to see that those constituencies had an advocate—a friend at court, as it were. Except for such advocacy, as both secular and ecclesiastical history have shown, such groups would have been relegated to the invisibility of which African American novelist Ralph Ellison wrote so compellingly in *Invisible Man*:

> I am invisible, understand, simply because people refuse to see me. . . . When they approach me they see only my surroundings, themselves, or figments of their imagination—indeed, everything and anything except me. . . . That invisibility to which I refer occurs because of a peculiar disposition of . . . their *inner* eyes, those eyes with which they look through their physical eyes upon reality.[1]

Let me give you an example of this invisibility. Immediately prior to joining the presiding bishop's staff, I served on the Standing Commission on World Mission of the Episcopal Church. I presume that one of the reasons I was appointed to that position was that I had begun my ministry as an overseas mission-

ary in Honduras, where I was ordained to the priesthood. At a meeting in Miami, we were asked to review
a draft of a forthcoming publication on missionaries.
I saw that there were biographical sketches of such
luminaries as John Henry Hobart, an early bishop of
New York; Samuel Isaac Joseph Schereschewsky, missionary to China who translated the Bible and parts of
the prayer book into Chinese; and James Hannington
and his companions, missionaries who were martyred
in Uganda. I politely asked why there was no mention
of James Theodore Holly, founder of the church in
Haiti and the first black bishop in the Episcopal
Church; Samuel Ferguson, an African American who
became bishop of Liberia; or Alexander Crummell,
intellectual, missionary to Liberia, and founder of St.
Luke's Church in Washington, D.C.[2] The sin of omis-
sion was compounded by the chairman's reply: "Well,
I suppose everyone will want to include his favorite
missionaries!" Had I not been present and arranged to
have further work done, the booklet on missionaries
would have gone forward, and all of its biographies
would have been of white men.

Incidents like this show that racism in the church
is, more often than not, unintentional—the result not
of malice but of unthinking behavior. Furthermore,
those responsible for such behavior usually do not
appreciate its seriousness or its impact on the person
it injures, and like the chairman of the commission,
they attempt to laugh it off. This incident also demonstrates that the victims of racism, not its perpetrators,
are often the people who are expected to seek and
effect redress. In other words, I had to identify the
problem, fight for its correction, and then (although I
was not responsible for the original error) provide the
means for correcting it.

Racial diversity on committees and commissions is often dismissed as pandering to political correctness. It is not. A commitment to inclusivity ensures that different ideas are brought to the table, thereby enriching both the experience of those who participate and the product they create. While it is true that African American Sunday school pupils reading the booklet on missionaries will derive a sense of pride from seeing black faces in it, it is also true that the horizons of white children will be broadened as well. They will benefit from knowing that not all in authority are white and that black people can fill positions of leadership, too.

Fifteen years later, a similar situation occurred. At a clergy leadership conference at which sixteen people were present (of whom I was the sole African American), a group of us were engaged in the usual dinner-time banter not uncommon among clergy at such gatherings. I was reminiscing with one of the bishops at the table about the amusing incidents that punctuated the episcopal election process in which we both had been candidates. At this point, a retired priest at the table said to me, "You must have felt like a mule in the Kentucky Derby. You couldn't have won, but at least you were in good company." The table was stunned into silence, and after an awkward hiatus, during which I chose not to address the issue, dinner was resumed. Later, I had a private conversation with the priest, and ultimately the matter was resolved when he, at my insistence, reluctantly made a public apology. Although the incident was both more painful and more personal than the occurrence at the committee meeting in Miami, they both had much in common: neither was initiated with any malice (in the circles in which the elderly cleric moved, such comments were apparently well within the boundaries of good-natured humor); it was dismissed as unimportant when the matter was brought up ("It was meant as a joke" and "I don't think of you as black" were some of the comments offered in defense); and I not only had to point out the impropriety but also had to devise a means for resolving it.

Another incident illustrates that racism in the church is not just personal, but institutional. I sit on the board of the *Anglican Theological Review*. At a meeting held at Seabury-Western Theological Seminary in Evanston, Illinois, a flyer was handed out listing local congregations at which members of the board might wish to worship on Sunday morning. A parish in a neighboring suburb and all but one of the parishes in Evanston were listed. The parish that was omitted was St. Andrew's, an African American congregation. Whoever compiled the list had clearly decided that members of the *ATR* board, most of whom were white, would not be interested in attending St. Andrew's. That action was apparently motivated by a belief that whites would not feel welcome or comfortable in a black church, or that they would not want to venture into a black neighborhood. The decision to omit St. Andrew's was also the result of ignorance about why black congregations are in existence—most having been created *not* by African Americans seeking to be separatist, but by whites who did not want to worship with them. After I brought this problem to the attention of the editors of the *ATR*, they concurred with my assessment of the situation, and suggested that I write an article about the incident.[3]

It was during the ordination process in the late 1960s that I was first conscious of experiencing racism. I say that neither as an indictment of the church nor for its shock value, but simply as a matter of fact. This statement, moreover, says as much about my own upbringing as it does about the Episcopal Church. I am a cradle Episcopalian. My grandparents emigrated to the United States early in the last century from the Caribbean island of Barbados, and they brought their Anglican faith with them. I was baptized in St. Philip's Church in Brooklyn, New York, where the priests and all two thousand members were black. At St. Philip's I received Sunday school and confirmation instruction, and served as an altar boy, chorister, and president of what was then called the Young People's Fellowship. Because of the example and urging of the parish clergy (who became my role models), and thanks to the encouragement of a corps of faithful laypeople, my vocation to the priesthood was nurtured. As a newly-minted postulant, I presented myself for an interview at the Berkeley Divinity School at Yale. After pleasantries, the priest/professor who interviewed me asked a startling question (which I later came to understand as a pastoral overture intended as a reality check): "Mr. Lewis, did it ever occur to you that the Episcopal Church doesn't particularly like you?" I literally did not understand the question. The Episcopal Church that I knew certainly liked me. So I responded with an emphatic "no."

What I did not understand at the time was that the professor was not speaking about Harold Lewis personally. Instead, he was speaking about the historical discrimination and marginalization of blacks in the Episcopal Church, about which I thankfully knew nothing. I say "thankfully" because such prior knowledge might have discouraged me from seeking holy orders, thus depriving me of the fulfilling ministry I have enjoyed. I also knew nothing about discrimination in the deployment of black clergy. And I knew nothing about how Absalom Jones, the first black priest in the Episcopal Church, was ordained in 1802 with the understanding that neither he nor his parish (St. Thomas', Philadelphia) would seek affiliation with the diocese of Pennsylvania. Needless to say, Jones and his predicament received no mention at all in the church history courses I took during my three years at seminary.

My first clue about this pattern of racism in the church came when the bishop of Long Island released me from his diocese in the spring of my senior year. As I later learned, there were no curacies that were open at that time to black ordinands in the diocese. Paul Washington, who for twenty-five years served as rector of the Church of the Advocate in Philadelphia, relates a similar story in his autobiography. He recalls that when he was a student (and the first black resident of the dormitory) at Philadelphia Divinity School in the 1940s, the Episcopal Hospital in Philadelphia refused to admit him to the clinical pastoral education program. Upon graduation, he was also told by the Overseas Department of the denomination that there were no missionary openings that an African American priest could fill. Later he was sent to Liberia only because Bravid Harris, the bishop of Liberia, was black and personally interceded on his behalf.[4]

I am a sixth-generation Anglican, and thus when I entered Yale Divinity School I was unprepared for questions from my black Baptist and African Methodist Episcopal colleagues about why I belonged to a "white church." I soon learned about the view, shared by many across racial and denominational lines, that there is something anomalous about being both black and Episcopalian. People subscribed to that idea, in part, because vast numbers of blacks fled the Episcopal Church after the Civil War and sought to join black-led denominations. Even the aphorism (usually attributed to Booker T. Washington) still carries force today: if a black man is anything but a Baptist or a Methodist, then someone has been tampering with his religion. This notion also holds sway in academic as well as popular circles, for C. Eric Lincoln, the preeminent scholar of African American religion, virtually excludes black Episcopalians from his monumental study, *The Black Church in the African American Experience.*[5]

While I had heard of discrimination and prejudice, I cannot remember ever having heard the word "racism" before I entered seminary. As I was to learn later, racism is more than simply prejudice or discrimination, for it involves the *power* of the dominant race to institutionalize its assumptions about being inherently superior. I saw this clearly during an event in which I participated when I was on the presiding bishop's staff. We had a "racism awareness day," and we all assembled at St. Bartholomew's Church in New York City to hold a series of workshops, seminars, role-plays, and plenary gatherings. In one session, we were asked to separate into two groups—whites and people of color. We were further asked to describe our respective experiences as members of those groups. The white group returned to report that its members did not give a thought to their racial identity. It was natural and normal—an idea that was consistently reinforced on billboards and in television commercials. People of color, on the other hand, never lost consciousness of their race. They were aware, on an almost daily basis, that their race could well be a factor in such everyday activities as interviewing for a job, shopping in a store, or hailing a taxi. Such apprehensions, moreover, were never absent from their professional interactions in the work of the church.

∿ The African American Struggle

While it is not within the scope of this book to treat in detail the complete history of race relations in the Episcopal Church, a broad outline will help us understand how cultural norms have affected the church's attitudes toward race and made possible the various incidents recounted above. The Episcopal Church traces its roots to the early sixteenth-century English settlement at Jamestown—the city that became the port of entry of the first slave ships into America at roughly the same time as the Church of England was established as the official religion of the Virginia colony. The nature of the relationship between Anglicanism and the Virginia government made the church a party to slavery at the outset. Prominent landowners and slaveholders, therefore, provided most of the lay leadership in the church. It was virtually impossible for any church member to oppose that nefarious institution, even if he or she had a mind to do so. As Samuel Wilberforce (the bishop of Oxford and William's son) later observed, American Anglicanism "raises no voice against the predominant evil; she palliates it in theory; and in practice she shares in it."[6]

The Society for the Propagation of the Gospel in Foreign Parts (SPG) was founded in 1701 with the dual purpose of providing chaplaincies for English settlers overseas and of evangelizing African slaves. According to historian Carleton Hayden, the SPG accepted slavery as a necessary factor in British prosperity—a prosperity, after all, that helped underwrite the organization's activities—and thus it strove to represent the planters' financial interests in that matter.[7] As a result of such collusion, the church raised no official objection when the Virginia legislature voted to reverse English common law by making the legal status of children born to a female slave and male planter depend not on the father, but on the mother. SPG missionaries instructed slaves in "the faith" (or a version of it), but when those men and women were baptized, the white evangelists usually reminded them of the limits of the sacrament's effectiveness. While baptism freed a person's *soul* from sin, it was commonly said, it did not free slaves from the duties owed to their earthly masters. This view was even given official sanction by Edmund Gibson, the bishop of London. In response to a query from planters in Virginia as to whether manumission necessarily had to accompany baptism, Gibson assured the slaveholders (in language reminiscent of Paul's epistle to Philemon) that baptism had no effect at all on the outward condition of those who were held as civil property.[8]

Owing to the establishment of chapels where slaves were evangelized, the black communicant strength of the Episcopal Church in the south before the Civil War was considerable. Approximately half the membership of the diocese of South Carolina, about forty percent of the communicant strength in Virginia, and a third of the church's membership in Georgia were black. However, the proportion of white-to-black membership changed drastically after the Civil War, when the Episcopal Church experienced a wholesale exodus of its black members. The dire nature of the situation was summed up in a report at the 1877 General Convention: while South Carolina alone claimed more than three thousand black souls in 1860, not even one-half of that number could be found in *all* the dioceses of the church, north and south, in the mid-1870s. Former slaves, understandably, did not wish to continue their affiliation with a church that had not only supported slavery but also used religion as a means to subjugate and control black people. Most former slaves, therefore, flocked to churches where they would be free of white domination and could enjoy the benefits of leadership by fellow African Americans. Black clerical leadership, on the other hand, was woefully absent from the Episcopal Church. From the time of the ordination of Absalom Jones until the end of the Civil War, only twenty-five black men were ordained priests; eighteen of them were sent to the mission fields in Africa, and most of the rest served black congregations in the north. If there had been more black clergy available at the end of the Civil War, a greater number of former slaves might well have remained within the Episcopal Church.

The denomination did make efforts to replenish the ranks of black Episcopalians through the establishment of the Freedman's Commission in 1865. The whites who founded that organization (renamed the Commission of Home Missions to Colored People in 1868) wanted to provide African Americans in the south with education, both practical and religious, in the hope that some of them might return to the Episcopal Church and become leaders of black congregations in it. This effort, as it turned out, bore little fruit—a failure that may be attributed to several basic flaws in the church's strategy.

The first problem concerned the propensity of whites to see the freed men and women not as an integral part of the American landscape, but as an alien group that had to be "won for Christ." The evangelization of African Americans was approached almost as if they constituted an overseas constituency, calling "from many an ancient river, from many a palmy plain "to be delivered "from error's chain"—to quote Reginald Heber's famous missionary hymn.[9]

Second, in attempting to provide for former slaves, whites displayed a patronizing attitude that tended to foster resistance in blacks. Third, the reluctance of white Episcopalians in the south to underwrite the program meant that the funding necessary for such a grandiose plan was never forthcoming. The fourth flaw was the whites' mistaken assumption that the "problem" of the black race in America could be solved simply by eradicating "ignorance." In effect, the architects of the Freedman's Commission were unable to deal with the existential realities of the situation in the south, where the white power structure adamantly refused to facilitate blacks' transition from bondage to freedom. And since the Episcopal Church itself had been unwilling either to condemn slavery or to recognize the equality of all Americans, most blacks knew they had been consistently victimized by the same denomination that was now making an effort to minister to them.

It is easy for us now to see the inconsistency of a church that gave lip service to incorporating people of African descent into its fellowship, while at the same time remaining unswervingly committed to segregationist policies at every level of its life. At a conference held at Sewanee, Tennessee in July 1883, for instance, a group of bishops, clergy, and leading lay men from southern dioceses produced a plan (which they submitted as a proposed canon at the 1883 General Convention) that would have disenfranchised all black communicants and placed them in a separate ecclesiastical jurisdiction under a white bishop. Responding vigorously to the "Sewanee canon," Alexander Crummell organized a group of African American church members (later called the Conference of Church Workers Among Colored People) in opposition to the whites' proposal. Crummell and his colleagues were successful in their efforts, for despite winning approval in the House of Bishops, the proposed canon did not gain the concurrence of the House of Deputies.

After failing at the national level, several southern bishops chose instead to institute in their own dioceses the segregation plan they had devised at the Sewanee meeting. During the late nineteenth century, therefore, as "Jim Crow" laws went into effect in all the southern states, dioceses in the south created "colored convocations" of African American Episcopalians. Subordinate to diocesan conventions, those convocations represented a parallel church structure in which black clergy and laity (who were not allowed to participate in the affairs of their diocesan convention) could meet. This system was not officially ended until 1954, when South Carolina became the last diocese to abolish its "colored convocation."

∽ **The Civil Rights Movement**

At the dawn of the twentieth century, the Episcopal Church had to come to grips with the fact that its evangelistic efforts had not brought about the desired results. While touting its missionary inroads in such places as the Philippines, China, and Japan, the church conceded that it still could not solve (what whites called) "the Negro Problem" at home. In a new attempt to remedy the situation, a group of white church members—bishops, priests, and lay men interested in black education—founded the American Church Institute for Negroes in 1906. This organization, however, was no more successful in ministering to African Americans than the agencies that preceded it. Since the denomination's confusion and paralysis were products of the paternalism present in society as a whole, little progress could be made throughout the first half of the twentieth century. In fact, as late as

1949, General Convention *failed* to pass a resolution allowing "equal rights and status" in worship and in parochial membership to people of all races, colors, and nationalities![10]

John Booty, historiographer of the Episcopal Church, aptly describes the civil rights movement as the time when white Episcopalians were "jolted out of their complacency" about the inequities in American society. Sit-in demonstrations, urban riots and incidents of unrest during the "long hot summers" of the 1960s, and the murders of civil rights workers (including Episcopal seminarian Jonathan Daniels) forced the church not only to address social issues but also to recognize the deep-seated racial prejudices within its midst.[11] In the wake of the historic *Brown v. Board of Education* decision of 1954, which mandated the desegregation of public schools, the church began to see how many of its own institutional practices had led to the oppression of racial minorities.

The Supreme Court decision was doubtless a factor affecting the decision of Presiding Bishop Henry Knox Sherrill to change the venue of the 1955 General Convention. Although the convention was scheduled to convene in Houston, the bishop of Texas was unable to guarantee that African American deputies would be housed in desegregated hotels. A delegation that included Tollie Caution, the priest in charge of "Negro Work" on the national church staff, and Thurgood Marshall, a member of St. Philip's Church in Harlem (and later a justice of the Supreme Court), persuaded Sherrill to move the site of the convention to Honolulu. Not surprisingly, the 1955 convention issued the strongest statement on race that the denomination had made up to that time. Declaring that "discrimination and segregation are contrary to the mind of Christ and the will of God," the statement urged Episcopalians to "accept and support the ruling of the Supreme Court and to anticipate constructively the local implementation of this ruling as the law of the land."[12] A year later, staff members of the national church issued a new edition of the denomination's "Guiding Principles for Negro Work," which called for the full integration of the races in all congregations, institutions, and agencies of the Episcopal Church.

In the preceding paragraphs, I have concentrated on the official actions and reactions of the Episcopal Church. While those activities give us an accurate view of the mind of the institutional church on racial matters in the twentieth century, they are by no means the entire story. In fact, as we have seen in other arenas of social justice, the concerns and expressions of indignation among rank-and-file church members are often critical factors in changing the views of the denominational leadership.

The Episcopal Society for Cultural and Racial Unity (ESCRU), for instance, was founded in 1959 out of frustration with the caution that many of the church's bishops had demonstrated on social issues. ESCRU was an independent, grassroots organization that soon gained a reputation for its unabashed denunciation of racial injustice in church and society. Its leaders envisioned ESCRU as the conscience of the church, prodding official bodies to become more racially inclusive. For the eleven years that elapsed between its founding at St. Augustine's College in 1959 and its demise in 1970, ESCRU protested discriminatory policies in the areas of employment and housing, opposed school segregation (especially in church-run institutions) and segregation laws in the south, and supported individual Episcopalians in their struggle for civil rights at the local level. In an innovative variation on the sit-in movement, ESCRU also sponsored "kneel-ins" in an effort to end segregation in Episcopal congregations. One of the organization's most controversial actions was an Ash Wednesday book burning, in which church school materials deemed to be racist in content were publicly set on fire.

As its name implied, ESCRU took pride in being an interracial organization, but from the outset its leadership was dominated by whites. By mid-1965, therefore, the society showed signs of having served its usefulness as ESCRU members began to wonder whether a largely white organization could either effectively attack racism or assist the empowerment of African Americans in the Episcopal Church. Eventually, because of the growing emphasis on the concept of "black power" in all civil rights organizations, ESCRU itself divided into two caucuses—one black, one white—at its annual meeting in 1968. As a product of the civil rights movement, the society had once been passionately committed to racial integration. Although the new emphasis on ethnic pride and racial diversity that emerged in the late 1960s forced the ESCRU leadership to shift gears, neither white advocates of integration nor African American proponents of black power were particularly motivated to keep the organization afloat any longer. Short of both funds and participants, ESCRU quietly disbanded in 1970. At the final gathering of the organization, its vice-president, Barbara Harris, urged ESCRU members to continue the struggle against racism—whites in the communities where they lived, and blacks within the newly formed Union of Black Episcopalians (UBE).

To say that the UBE rose like a phoenix from the ashes of ESCRU would be only partially true. The UBE has a long and distinguished lineage that began with the formation of the Conference of Church Workers

Among Colored People as an advocacy group for black Episcopalians in the nineteenth century. Although the church's apparent commitment to racial integration led to the disbanding of the Conference in the mid-1960s, black clergy soon noted that little change had actually occurred in the sphere of clergy deployment—African Americans were still being treated as virtual outsiders within their own denomination. After a series of unsuccessful meetings about this problem with various white bishops, a group of African American clergy met at St. Philips', Harlem in early 1968 and organized what eventually became known as the UBE. From the outset, the UBE was an amalgam of disparate groups—disillusioned former ESCRU members, traditional work-within-the-system black Episcopalians, and recently ordained clergy emboldened and inspired by the civil rights and black power movements. What held the organization together was the belief that only a strong, united black voice could exert the pressure necessary to bring about the needed changes in the church, especially the eradication of racism.

ESCRU and the UBE, though ideologically dissimilar, were grassroots movements founded on a belief in racial equality. They were both born of impatience, an impatience that caused them to challenge the official structures of the church to live out the claims of the gospel in the arenas of racial and social justice. If the two organizations proved to be more successful than earlier organizations and individuals, it was because of the external pressure of the civil rights movement, which served to motivate the church to come to grips with the sin of racism.

∿ Other Racial Ethnic Groups

As both the title and content of Andrew Hacker's 1992 book, *Two Nations: Black and White, Separate, Hostile, Unequal,* would suggest, the race issue in the United States has usually been defined, for plausible historical reasons, in terms of relationships between blacks and whites. Despite this fact, we also live in a multiracial and multicultural society, and demographic projections inform us that by the third decade of this century the term "minority group" will become a misnomer. As we look at the ministry of the Episcopal Church among ethnic minorities over the past one hundred years, therefore, we see distinct parallels with its "colored work" program of the nineteenth century—the leadership of the church first determining that it will minister to those groups as distinct cultural entities, and then gradually over time welcoming them into the ecclesiastical "mainstream."

Throughout its history, the Episcopal Church has attempted to develop ministries to various racial ethnic groups as the need has arisen. Under the aegis of the SPG, for instance, the church began to work concurrently among Native Americans and black slaves. But whereas the mission to blacks was predicated upon the idea of convincing them that the master-slave relationship was divinely ordained, the Christianization of the Indians was started in an attempt to bring an end to what was deemed their "savage" behavior. According to a 1680 document, conversion to Christianity would not only help reduce the risk of insurrection in the native population, but also teach the Indians about the alleged superiority of English culture. In the end, the evangelization of Native Americans was a powerful instrument for "making men to forget their own people, and their

Father's house, and joining them in affection to the most distant strangers."[13]

Missionaries to Indian tribes encountered many obstacles. Not only were the barriers of language and custom and the occasional threats of war a problem, but missionary work was also impeded when the United States government initiated the forced migration of Native American tribes to reservations in the nineteenth century. Despite those difficulties, the 1870s witnessed a surge of missionary work in the west, and during the same period in which the church established the Freedman's Commission, it established an Indian Commission as part of its board of missions. This action resulted in the election of William Hobart Hare as bishop of Niobrara, a jurisdiction that would eventually encompass all of South Dakota. During his episcopate, Hare confirmed more than seven thousand people, and today nearly half of the communicants in the diocese of South Dakota are Native Americans. The church was also successful in founding schools and in raising up candidates for the ordained ministry. More recent developments include the establishment of Navajoland, a missionary district for the Native Americans of New Mexico, Arizona, and Utah.

In some ways, the church's Hispanic ministries began by default. Until the 1950s, the Church of England maintained missions in Guatemala, Honduras, El Salvador, Costa Rica, and British Honduras (now Belize). Anglicans in these areas were mostly West Indians who had migrated from Jamaica, Barbados, St. Vincent, and other Caribbean islands to work for the fruit companies that held sway in Central America. When the Episcopal Church inherited jurisdiction over those countries and formed the missionary diocese of Central America in 1957, it began to reach out to the indigenous populations. The church also created Province IX in 1964 in order that other dioceses in Latin America could work toward greater autonomy. When I served in Honduras in the early 1970s, only one of the half-dozen congregations, all served by clergy from abroad, had services in Spanish. Today, there are virtually no services in English, and the majority of the more than one hundred congregations in the diocese are served by native clergy.

In the United States, the church's Hispanic ministries have focused on immigrants from Puerto Rico, the Dominican Republic, Mexico, and other Spanish-speaking countries in Central America and the Caribbean. As is the case with the Hispanic population in general, the number of Hispanic Episcopalians has increased considerably since the first wave of immigrants arrived in this country in the 1940s. By the 1990s Americans of Hispanic origin were the fastest-growing ethnic group in the church, and the number of those preparing for the Episcopal priesthood rivals the number seeking ordination in the Roman Catholic Church.[14] Most Hispanic missioners now have the responsibility not only to minister to existing congregations, but also to reach out to new immigrants. Part of their role, too, has been educational—creating bridges of understanding between Hispanic and "Anglo" Episcopalians, and celebrating the contributions of Hispanics within the Episcopal Church.

Among the earliest ministries to Asian Americans were the True Sunshine Mission for Chinese Americans, begun in San Francisco in 1905, and the Japanese Mission that was opened in the same city eleven years later. Comparable ministries to those on the west coast developed in the New York City area in succeeding decades. Because the church's work among Asian Americans has been limited to areas with a sizeable Asian American population, it has usually been on a smaller scale than has been the case in regard to other racial minorities. Like the Hispanic ministries, however, some dioceses have appointed missioners to increase the church's outreach. The attitudes of the broader society toward the Asian American community has been another limiting factor. The internment policy instituted by the United States government against Japanese Americans during World War II did much to heighten racist, anti-Asian sentiment in this country, and it may well have had an indirect influence on the church's policy.

∽ Signs of Hope

I shall end this chapter as I began it, on a personal note. On July 2, 1996, the *Pittsburgh Post-Gazette* carried the headline, "White Episcopal Parish Calls Black Rector." It told of my call to be the fifteenth rector of Calvary Church, a predominantly white congregation and the largest parish in the city of Pittsburgh. This article actually fulfilled the prophecy of Robert Hood, who wrote in 1990 that it was still "newsworthy in the Episcopal Church when a black gets elected . . . rector of a white parish."[15] Such decisions by vestries, thankfully, are becoming less and less newsworthy. Parishes such as St. Mark's, Capitol Hill, in Washington, D.C.; St. Augustine's in Santa Monica, California; St. Michael's in New York City; and St. Alban's in Augusta, Georgia are among several predominantly white parishes that have called African Americans to their pulpits within the past five years. At least three cathedrals, including Washington's National Cathedral, have black deans. And the first year of the new millennium witnessed the consecrations of two African American bishops, Wendell Gibbs as coadjutor of Michigan and Michael Curry as bishop of North Carolina. Bishop Curry's consecration marked the first of an African American in the south since Edward Thomas Demby and Henry Beard Delany were consecrated as suffragan bishops for colored work in 1918.

Of even greater significance is the changing face of parishes themselves. Gone are the days when a "c" (for "colored") appeared in the *Episcopal Church Annual* next to the names of predominantly black congregations. In large cities and sprawling suburbs in virtually every part of the country, all-white parishes have become a rarity. It is heartening that the Episcopal Church now recognizes the gifts that black clergy bring to the table and is breaking out of the earlier paradigm that relegated black clergy solely to work in black congregations. It is encouraging, too, that the "kneel-ins" sponsored by ESCRU in the 1960s are no longer necessary, as people of color are warmly welcomed in many predominantly white parishes.

Having helped to develop and implement national church policy under two presiding bishops, and having attended virtually every General Convention since 1970, I have learned in the first four years of my rectorship that posters and slogans produced at the Episcopal Church Center in New York, like convention resolutions and proclamations decrying racism, pale beside the experience of clergy and people working out their own salvation, learning from each other as children of God, as fellow pilgrims along the way. We must together attempt to "take away all hatred and prejudice, and whatever else may hinder us from godly union and concord...so we may be all of one heart and of one soul, united in one holy bond of truth and peace" (BCP 818).

~ Chapter Six

Gender

The church still has a long way to go in its ability to recognize and affirm the leadership abilities of women. Women need not be regarded as inter-changeable with men, but their experiences and perspectives, often different from men's, can enrich the whole and enhance the calibre of leadership for the whole church.

—Committee for the Full Participation
of Women in the Church,
Reaching Toward Wholeness: The Participation
of Women in the Episcopal Church

There is considerable irony in the fact that it was necessary in the 1980s to establish a body called the Committee for the Full Participation of Women in the Church. Women, after all, have quietly but consistently dominated the church's life at the local level across the spectrum of denominations. As Baptist minister Peter Gomes of Harvard University's Memorial Church observes, "The program for most churches is managed and supplied by women, initiatives in religious education and works of charity have long been the special province of women, and the moral and religious influences of home life have historically been shaped by women."[1] However, despite the many important roles that women have played in American religious affairs over the centuries, there was once a time—only a few years ago—when they held a decidedly subordinate position in the governing structures of the Episcopal Church.

~ The Woman's Auxiliary

When I was growing up at St. Philip's, Brooklyn in the early 1950s, my mother, aunts, and grandmother belonged to something called the Woman's Auxiliary. "Auxiliary" was a big word for a little boy. I had no idea what it meant, but I assumed it must be something very important. I did not know then that "auxiliary" is defined as "offering or providing help" and "functioning in a subsidiary capacity." I also did not know of the vision of Mary Emery (the first national secretary of the Woman's Auxiliary) and of her sister, Julia (the second national secretary): maintaining an organization for women that would support the church's missionary activities through education, financial giving, and prayer. If it is true that we lived in a man's world back then, it was no less true that we were members of a man's church. A female priest was an oxymoron, a woman bishop unthinkable. I even remember listening to an acolyte warden give a theological treatise on the unsuitability of girls as altar servers! Still, the women in my family took their membership in the Woman's Auxiliary very seriously. Although most members of the Auxiliary accepted the status quo in the church, they were also conscious of the valuable role that women could play even within a conservative system.

A few years later, when women's ministries began to be recognized as useful in their own right, the organization was rebaptized the General Division of Women's Work at the national level, and local units were named Episcopal Church Women (ECW). Although the ECW continued to function at the parish level in ways similar to the Auxiliary's work—most notably, by raising funds for foreign and domestic missions through the United Thank Offering—the decision to change the name was highly significant. It symbolized the desire of women to work together with men as equal partners in the ministry of the Episcopal Church. According to a resolution passed at the 1958 meeting of the General Convention (an all-male institution at that time), women were to be respected as "an important and integral part of every aspect of the Church's life."[2] While that hardly seems like a remarkable statement today, it does reveal how attitudes about the place of women in American society had begun to change by the late 1950s.

As with other historically disenfranchised groups discussed in this book, women were once denied access to official positions of power and influence in the Episcopal Church. The theological views on which this treatment was based depended upon the interpretation of a handful of biblical passages that portrayed women as submissive, powerless, and, above all, inferior to men. Two assertions from the Pauline epistles are probably the most often quoted. The first is unambiguous:

> Women should be silent in the churches. For they are not permitted to speak, but should be subordinate. . . . If there is anything they desire to know, let them ask their husbands at home. For it is shameful for a woman to speak in church. (1 Corinthians 14:34–35)

The complementary passage in Paul's first letter to Timothy reiterates this idea:

> Let a woman learn in silence with full submissiveness. I permit no woman to teach or to have authority over a man; she is to keep silent. (1 Timothy 2:11-12)

Such statements about the submissive status of women, however, clearly represent a minority position in the scriptures. The Old Testament, for instance, is replete with stories about such powerful and influential women as the prophet Miriam (Exodus 15:20-21) and Deborah, a judge of Israel (Judges 4:4). The New Testament mentions, among others, the ministries of Lydia (Acts 16:14), Phoebe (a deacon and colleague of Paul—Romans 16:1-2), and Priscilla (Romans 16:3). Indeed, the women who followed Jesus were the first to see him after his resurrection (Matthew 28:1-10). It is noteworthy, therefore, that the Bible's "minority report" on the status of women could hold sway for almost two millennia. This clearly shows the tremendous power that the secular culture has in shaping attitudes within the church.

As I have suggested above, it is important to remember the fact that women, while denied access to *official* positions of power, were never without influence in everyday church life—a reality that I think has parallels with the experiences of black Episcopalians. Although both African Americans and women were prevented from exercising authority at the highest levels in the Episcopal Church, those groups exercised significant influence at the local level and within the spheres in which they were allowed to exercise responsibility. Thus, by operating independently of the clergy and on the periphery of official denominational affairs, the leadership of the Woman's Auxiliary was able to mobilize the energy and imagination of thousands of Episcopal women. As historian Pamela W. Darling observes, the Auxiliary became "a shadow organization within which women could participate quasi-autonomously," thereby circumventing the often cumbersome machinery of the male-dominated church bureaucracy.[3] Women established formidable networks and served the church in numerous capacities. Like racial minority groups, they were able to accomplish a good deal without ever challenging or directly threatening the established system.

∽ Religious Orders and Deaconesses

In addition to the activities of the Auxiliary, Episcopal women wielded considerable power through the various religious orders that were inspired by the rise of the Oxford Movement in the mid-nineteenth century. Despite renouncing all the outward and visible signs of power through their vows of poverty, chastity, and obedience, members of the female religious orders not only helped redefine the roles of women in society but were also on the cutting edge of ministry in the church. In fact, because of the social ministries that many of the sisterhoods performed in the late nineteenth century, groups that would not otherwise have received the attention of the Episcopal Church were evangelized: German immigrants on the Lower East Side of New York; impoverished blacks in Baltimore; poor girls, black and white, whose education would normally have been overlooked; orphans and physically disabled children; and prostitutes and battered women, to name only a few. Having rejected the social roles ordinarily expected of women in the middle and upper classes, Episcopal nuns proved to be pioneers who demonstrated the ability of women to function as professionals by managing large institutions, supervising employees, and developing educational programs.[4]

Another similarity between the parallel struggles of women and African Americans was that each group was willing to accept ostensibly inferior roles in order to place a "foot in the door" of the official church leadership. Like African American clergy engaged in various aspects of "colored work" in southern dioceses in the early twentieth century, women were given an opportunity to acquit themselves in "lesser" roles within the church hierarchy. Thus, beginning with the passage of the deaconess canon at the 1889 General Convention, some women were allowed to be trained and "set apart" as professional church workers. After the office of deaconess was approved at the national level, educational programs were established in order to prepare women to serve in that capacity. Supported through the United Thank Offering, deaconess training schools were opened in New York City and in Philadelphia, and rigorous courses in biblical studies, theology, and church history were offered alongside classes in tailoring, nursing, and household management. Susan Knapp, dean of the New York Training School for Deaconesses, became the chief spokesperson of this movement in the United States. After meeting with many of the founders of the deaconess movement in England, Knapp crafted the American program on models she had observed in the English church. Thanks to her efforts, the number of American deaconesses grew to a high of 226 in 1922.

As historian Mary Donovan notes, the clergy involved in the establishment of the deaconess movement saw the program they developed as a religious extension of the Victorian ideals of true womanhood. Those male leaders believed that all women were inherently pious and domestic, and they wanted those whom they set apart as deaconesses to employ their natural nurturing tendencies in the church rather than in the home. In addition, since deaconesses were not allowed to marry, priests and bishops expected that those women would substitute obedience to *them* for obedience to a husband.[5] Most deaconesses, on the other hand, held a different view of their calling than the clergy who supported them, and they went beyond the gender-specific boundaries imposed by their culture. Although they certainly believed they were giving a public voice to the higher moral sensibilities they possessed as women, the deaconesses also saw themselves as professional church workers, educated in theological matters as well as in nursing and housekeeping. Indeed, they exercised a genuine religious vocation within the Episcopal Church during a period in which women's roles were otherwise quite circumscribed.[6]

Although male deacons and female deaconesses both shared a servant ministry, deaconesses had no liturgical function. Deaconesses, then, had much in common with nuns, for they had a recognized ecclesiastical role without being allowed to lead public worship on a regular basis. Deaconesses were also habited like nuns (albeit more simply than members of religious orders), and they took what amounted to a vow of celibacy. Despite the fact that the service for the setting apart of deaconesses referred to such stereotypically feminine qualities as "docility" and "meekness," the positions of responsibility with which they were entrusted gave those women an official status in the church. Later generations would build on the foundation laid by the deaconesses as they pressed for the full equality of women in the church.

～ Women Deputies

The manifold accomplishments of ordinary lay women, nuns, and deaconesses notwithstanding, the struggle of women for *political* recognition as deputies in the General Convention of the Episcopal Church is a story of fits and starts, of advances and setbacks, of pyrrhic victories and crushing defeats. General Convention statements in the early twentieth century had a penchant for combining lofty, laudatory platitudes with reminders that women should stay in their traditional place. Yet in the midst of such remarks, women seized upon the glimmers of hope that were offered them as a warrant to mount their campaign for inclusion. Thus, at a time when women's suffrage was being debated in secular political forums, the 1913 convention announced that it was "the policy of the whole Church to encourage the cooperation of women in all the activities of the Church, and to furnish all possible avenues for the expression of their zeal and devotion."[7] This declaration set the stage for the first serious attempt to make it possible for women to be seated as deputies, when a constitutional amendment calling for equal rights for women in the church was presented to the 1916 General Convention. The attitudes inherent in sexism and in the assumption of male privilege were so deeply rooted, however, that the resolution was simply dismissed as "inexpedient," with no further explanation offered at the time.[8]

Despite this rebuff in 1916, the idea of women's greater inclusion in church affairs began to gain a following. This emerging feminist sensibility within the church was significantly aided in 1920 when the lengthy struggle to win the ballot for American women succeeded, and the Nineteenth Amendment became part of the United States Constitution. That same year, the Lambeth Conference declared that women should be admitted on equal terms to all church councils. The male leaders of the Episcopal Church, however, still refused to see the wisdom of women's suffrage within decision-making bodies in their denomination, and discussions about the admission of women as deputies to General Convention came to a halt in the mid-1920s.

General Convention remained unchallenged as an all-male preserve until shortly after World War II. Because the war helped open new avenues for the participation of women in all aspects of American life, the diocese of Missouri was emboldened to elect Elizabeth Dyer as one of its four lay deputies to the 1946 convention. Although Dyer was seated when the convention began, a slender majority in the House of Deputies eventually ruled that the term "layman" was not gender-inclusive, but referred only to male communicants. Three other dioceses joined Missouri in resisting this decision by electing women deputies to the 1949 General Convention. However, when the meeting began that year, a solid majority of deputies voted to bar those women from participating in the convention.[9] This prohibition remained in effect until 1967, when at the same gathering that approved the creation of the General Convention Special Program, both the House of Deputies and the House of Bishops overwhelmingly endorsed the seating of women deputies—a change that was officially implemented at the 1970 convention.

Throughout this fifty-year struggle to gain both a voice and a vote in the House of Deputies, women in the Episcopal Church were not entirely without power or representation whenever the General Convention met. Following a practice akin to the separate "colored convocations" of black Episcopalians in southern dioceses, members of the Woman's Auxiliary assembled at their own ancillary Triennial meetings. This pattern was codified in 1880, when it was determined that representatives from auxiliaries in every diocese of the Episcopal Church would gather at the same time and location as the General Convention. (There was even a proposal for the establishment of a "House of Churchwomen" as a third component in the General Convention, but that idea never came to fruition.) Although women were confined to their own sphere, their voices began to grow stronger in the period between the two world wars, and starting in 1935, the Triennial was allowed to nominate four representatives to serve on the National Council (now the Executive Council) of the church. The Triennial also controlled the disbursal of funds from the United Thank Offering. It is significant, therefore, that the decision of the Episcopal Church Women to give $3 million to fight poverty and racism in American society *preceded* the House of Deputies' creation of the $9 million General Convention Special Program at the 1967 General Convention. The women's generosity and passion for social justice helped inspire the "official" actions later authorized by the male deputies at the convention. In addition, the leadership and financial influence that the Triennial exercised was surely a key factor when the 1967 gathering also voted to accept women as deputies.[10]

~ Ordained Ministries

It is not merely coincidental that the 1970 General Convention—the first convention at which women participated fully as deputies—amended the church canons in order to allow women to be ordained to the diaconate. The first serious discussion of this topic began in the fall of 1965, when James Pike, the decid-

edly unorthodox bishop of California, formally
invested Phyllis Edwards, a deaconess in his diocese,
with the symbols of the deacon's office. Since Pike and
Edwards were both active supporters of the civil rights
movement, they understood the importance of direct
action in confronting injustice. Despite the action they
took liturgically, it was not clear to the rest of the
denomination whether a deaconess could so easily be
transformed into a deacon. As a consequence,
Presiding Bishop John Hines appointed a Committee
to Study the Proper Place of Women in the Ministry of
the Church, asking it to present a report to the House
of Bishops in 1966.

After the committee reported that the church
should not only ordain woman as deacons, but should
consider ordaining them to the priesthood as well,
both the proponents and opponents of women's ordination began to mobilize their forces. The 1967
General Convention authorized the licensing of
women as lay readers, and after lobbying by those
who decried the exclusion of women from positions of
leadership in the church, the 1970 convention also
approved the training and ordination of women as
deacons.

These debates about the validity of women's ordination took place, moreover, within the context of
related discussions about the revision of the prayer
book. According to the Offices of Instruction in the
1928 prayer book, Episcopalians in the early twentieth century recognized three "orders of Ministers" in
the church: "Bishops, Priests, and Deacons" (1928 BCP,
294). However, the liturgical scholars who crafted the
"new" prayer book (approved initially at the 1976
General Convention and officially adopted three years
later) were strongly influenced by biblical and patristic concepts of the Christian ministry. Desiring to

restore the laity to their rightful place within the ministry of the church, the authors of the catechism in the 1979 prayer book affirmed a fourfold model: "The ministers of the Church are lay persons, bishops, priests, and deacons" (BCP 855). This inclusion of the laity not only reflected a biblical understanding of ministry as *diakonia*, but also symbolically freed the church from a male-only, hierarchical view of authority. As soon as women were deemed fit to exercise lay ministries—lay reader, chalice bearer, and deputy to General Convention—it became clear to most church members that there was no longer any inherent barrier—canonical, constitutional, theological, or rubrical—to keep them from being admitted to the ordained ministries as well. While it had taken the Episcopal Church nearly two hundred years to recognize the validity of women's lay ministries in national legislative assemblies, it took only a few more years to open the diaconate, priesthood, and episcopate to them.

Still, from the perspective of women seeking to be ordained in the early 1970s, the process was anything but simple or easy. Forty-two women were ordained to the diaconate in the period after the 1970 General Convention, and they fully expected that the ordination of women to the priesthood would be approved at the next convention. They were sorely disappointed, however. Following an emotional and acrimonious debate, the measure failed after a vote by orders in the House of Deputies at the 1973 convention.[11] In the wake of that parliamentary defeat, disappointment and resentment ran high among the women and their supporters. Soon, a group of women deacons and bishops began to discuss the possibility of ordaining women to the priesthood without waiting for the approval of General Convention. To that end, eleven women deacons were ordained to the priesthood on the feast of Saints Mary and Martha, July 24, 1974. The ordination took place in the Church of the Advocate in Philadelphia—a black congregation whose rector, Paul Washington, had distinguished himself as a civil rights activist. Three retired bishops—Daniel Corrigan, Robert DeWitt, and Edward Welles—and one still active diocesan bishop, Antonio Ramos of Costa Rica, officiated; Charles Willie, the first black man to hold the post of vice-president of the House of Deputies, was the preacher. Both the venue and the participants at the event were carefully and appropriately chosen, for the ordination was modeled after a civil rights protest. Those who were present in the Church of the Advocate that day were prepared to break an unjust law while appealing to a higher authority, namely (in Pamela Darling's words), a "conscience informed by the Holy Spirit, accountable to a community which valued the full humanity of women above the claims of ecclesiastical tradition."[12]

The validity of the Philadelphia ordinations (and of the four additional ordinations that took place in Washington, D.C. in 1975) was hotly debated in the church over the next two years. With the threat of schism close at hand, the 1976 General Convention passed a resolution affirming that the church's ordination canons applied to women as well as to men. In addition, the House of Bishops recognized that the ordinations of the "Philadelphia Eleven" and the "Washington Four" were "valid but irregular." Following a service of recognition and reconciliation, each of the fifteen irregularly ordained women would be duly licensed to exercise the office of priest in her diocese. Nevertheless, in an attempt to placate the substantial minority who had theological objections to the ordination of women, the bishops in 1977 passed a resolution allowing their colleagues both to disagree with the church's official position and to refuse to ordain or license women clergy in their dioceses. This so-called conscience clause, which was never ratified by General Convention, was formally overturned at the 1997 convention, when the church's canons affirming the ordination and deployment of women clergy were made mandatory in all dioceses of the Episcopal Church.

The ordinations that took place at the Church of the Advocate in Philadelphia were profound symbols of the social witness of the Christian church. The image I most remember from press reports of that service was the photograph of the altar frontal, designed by the women of the parish for the occasion. The words of Paul's letter to the Galatians were emblazoned on the frontal: "There is neither Jew nor Greek, there is neither slave nor free, there is neither male nor female; for you are all one in Christ Jesus" (3:28 RSV). In a press release announcing the event, the participants urged their friends and supporters to bring that Pauline promise into reality at the ordination service. The text was well chosen, especially since other writings of Paul were being cited as biblical warrant for *not* ordaining women. Unlike the often-quoted passages from 1 Corinthians and 1 Timothy, which reflect an uncritical acceptance of cultural norms in the first century, the Galatians passage affirms that the sacrament of baptism renders meaningless the categories used in secular society to categorize and classify people. Paul maintains that in Christ gender, race, religion, and nationality are made meaningless, for all who are baptized become "Abraham's offspring, heirs according to the promise" (Galatians 3:29).

This appeal to Galatians was more than a mere *quid pro quo* to refute the claims of those who had hurled other biblical writings against the women. By using Galatians as their battle cry, and by insisting that a doctrine of ministry based on gender was contrary to the egalitarian stance of the gospel, the advocates of women's ordination succeeded in refuting two major objections to their position: first, that there were valid theological, rather than simply cultural, arguments against ordaining women; and second, that women in the church were doing nothing more than riding piggyback on the secular women's liberation movement. Although traditionalists asserted that the *matter* of the sacraments was critical, and that the necessary "matter" for the ordination of a priest was a male human being—a bishop laying hands on a giraffe, some wags said, could not make that animal a priest—the Galatians argument undercut such philosophical reasoning by appealing to the plain words of scripture about the equality of all people in Christ. And while the second objection might have had some truth to it—the late 1960s and early 1970s were certainly a period of upheaval and soul-searching about historic injustices—the earliest Christians, too, felt themselves out of step with accustomed norms in their day. This sense of being a cultural outsider led Paul to proclaim the gospel's ability to overturn traditional expectations about the ordering of society.

In the period when women were first ordained as priests in the Episcopal Church, questions regarding the second-class citizenship experienced by both racial minorities and women were being raised on a daily basis throughout the United States. Among the people who linked the goals of the civil rights movement with those of the women's movement was African American lawyer and activist Pauli Murray. Murray had challenged segregation laws in the south in the 1940s, and in the early 1950s she edited a book,

States' Laws on Race and Color, that aided Thurgood
Marshall and NAACP lawyers in the key *Brown* school
desegregation decision. In December 1965, she and a
colleague published a law review article in which they
equated "Jane Crow" and Jim Crow, arguing that the
rights of women and the rights of African Americans
were "only different phases of the fundamental and
indivisible issue of human rights."[13] A year later, she
participated with Betty Friedan and other women in
the founding of the National Organization for
Women.

Murray was also an active Episcopalian, but in the
late 1960s she found herself increasingly at odds with
the rector and vestry of her parish in New York.
Incensed that women were not given a place of leadership in the church's worship services, she asked why
that privilege was not accorded to all Episcopalians
without regard to sex. "Suppose only white people did
these things? Or only Negroes?...We would see
immediately that the Church is guilty of grave discrimination," she asserted. As parishioners at her otherwise socially progressive parish began to debate the
issues that Murray raised, they discovered that male-
dominated worship was determined as much by custom and tradition as by church law. Energized by this
experience, Murray became active with other Episcopal
women at the national level in challenging male privilege in the sanctuary. Thus, in July 1974, she was
present in Philadelphia when one of the last barriers of
gender in her denomination was toppled. Especially
pleased that a black parish had hosted the event, she
noted the symbolic importance in the fact that "the
rejected opened their arms to the rejected."[14] In this
period Murray sensed that she, too, was called to the
ordained ministry, and on January 8, 1977 she

became the first African American woman to be ordained a priest in the Episcopal Church.

Barbara Clementine Harris was another black Episcopalian who recognized the relationship between the two freedom struggles. A warden of the Advocate in Philadelphia, she had been the crucifer at the historic 1974 ordinations. A few years later Harris studied for the ordained ministry and served as a priest in the diocese of Pennsylvania in the 1980s. She preached boldly about oppression and justice for the marginalized in society, and her considerable skills as an activist and pastor eventually led to her election as suffragan bishop of the diocese of Massachusetts in 1988. Harris' consecration was the last straw for many traditionalists in the Episcopal Church. I remember being in touch with Edward Rodman, canon missioner for minority communities in Massachusetts, in the weeks preceding Harris's consecration in February 1989. The consents from other dioceses (usually a formality) were coming in slowly, and at one point it was feared that her consecration service would have to be postponed. I also remember reading the impassioned letters to the church press objecting to her election and predicting that it would lead to schism in the church. And I remember being present as a eucharistic minister at the consecration itself, hearing the formal objections that were made. I later learned that both Harris and Presiding Bishop Edmond Browning had received death threats prior to the service, and some of the vested persons in the procession that day were, in fact, armed guards.

In 1999, Browning came out of retirement to celebrate the tenth anniversary of her consecration with Bishop Harris. In the decade that had elapsed, seven other women priests had been consecrated to the episcopate in the United States, along with three others elsewhere in the Anglican Communion. Despite the continued opposition of a few bishops and dioceses, the presence of women in the ordained ministry of the Episcopal Church is now accepted as a fact of life. Perhaps in this new millennium, as we all continue "to grow into the full stature of Christ" (BCP 302), Paul's passionate hope that ancient barriers between slave and free, Jew and Greek, male and female will at long last be abolished.

Chapter Seven

Human Sexuality

The turmoil in Christian churches over issues that have to do with sex and sexuality is hardly a blessing, but it need not be a wholly bad thing either. There has seldom been a time when Christians were not embroiled in one noisy dispute or another, and unedifying though the quarrels were, their result in the long run has been to refine and clarify what Christianity is and what it is for. If, as the adage says, the church is always getting reformed, its reformation seems to go hand in hand with controversy.

—Charles Hefling,
Our Selves, Our Souls and Bodies

While this chapter will deal principally with issues relating to homosexuality, the phrase "human sexuality" that appears in the title was purposely chosen. Homosexuality cannot be considered in a vacuum, and debates currently surrounding it must be seen in light of traditional understandings of sexuality in general. While the question of homosexuality has received what many consider an inordinate amount of attention, changing views on human sexuality have also affected the church's views on abortion, divorce, contraception, premarital sex, and even marriage itself. As ethicist Timothy F. Sedgwick observes, the current dialogue on sexuality in the Episcopal Church raises two separate but related questions. First, what are the purposes of sexual relationships? And second— the key one today— what are the responsibilities of the *church* in supporting such relationships? In other words, why should members of the church care about what people do sexually? This question goes to the heart not simply of human sexuality but of the Christian faith as well.[1]

Despite a strong, alternative tradition that has favored the state of celibacy (viewed by some as a superior state, owing to Jesus' own example), the church has consistently honored and supported the institution of marriage. Whenever a man and woman had sexual relations, they were expected to do so in an exclusive and lifelong relationship as husband and wife. Sex between persons who were not married to each other was deemed unacceptable. Often forbidden, too, was what was usually called the "solitary vice," a euphemism for masturbation. Such views envisioned human sexuality as primarily functional, tied to the divine commandment to "be fruitful and multiply" (Genesis 1:28). Marriage was also seen as an institution whose primary purpose was to strengthen society and to protect the children of such unions. Sexual pleasure and desire were factored into this equation only as necessary evils leading to a desirable end. Even companionship was not considered beneficial in itself, but was viewed merely as a by-product of the hearth and home in which children were raised.

Such traditional moral positions were predicated upon and grounded in biblical texts, particularly the creation stories in Genesis. The Celebration and Blessing of a Marriage in *The Book of Common Prayer* speaks to this scriptural understanding of the sacrament. When I prepare couples for marriage, I point to the clear biblical allusions in the opening exhortation:

> The bond and covenant of marriage was established by God in creation [Genesis 1:27], and our Lord Jesus Christ adorned this manner of life by his presence and first miracle at a wedding in Cana of Galilee [John 2:1-11]. It signifies to us the mystery of the union between Christ and his Church [Ephesians 5:31-32], and Holy Scripture commends it to be honored among all people. (BCP 423)

In recent years, however, both religious and secular views of the nature and purpose of human sexuality have undergone considerable change. Indeed, the words of the marriage service in the 1979 prayer book hint at one important aspect of that change, and they constitute a noticeable departure from the 1928 prayer book:

> The union of husband and wife in heart, body, and mind is intended by God for their mutual joy; for the help and comfort given one another in prosperity and adversity; and, when it is God's will, for the procreation of children and their nurture in the knowledge and love of the Lord. (BCP 423)

Note that "mutual joy" is listed as the primary reason for marriage. "Help and comfort" (that is, companionship) is now listed next, and procreation is listed as a third but nonessential purpose. While this clearly represents a shift in the church's understanding of marriage, the current teaching is still thoroughly biblical in its rationale. According to Timothy Sedgwick, Jesus' teaching on divorce in Mark's gospel—"So they are no longer two, but one flesh. Therefore, what God has joined together, let no one separate" (10:8-9)—establishes the fundamental equality between men and women, thus emphasizing the primacy of companionship over procreation in marriage.[2] This, as we shall see, bears relevance to the discussion of homosexuality, for some people are now arguing that the companionship gay and lesbian couples exhibit and the love and care they feel for each other should likewise be recognized and blessed by the church.

～ Homosexuality and the Episcopal Church

While the Episcopal Church has always had many homosexual members, both lay and ordained, only in the recent years have many gays and lesbians ceased being silent about their orientation and begun to ask for open acceptance. (This situation parallels what has occurred in American society generally since the "Stonewall riot" of 1969—the event that marks the advent of the gay liberation movement.) In response to the sexual revolution of the late 1960s, Episcopalians first sympathetically addressed the question of homosexuality at official levels in a report produced at the 1967 General Convention. Although the convention report identified Genesis 1:27 ("male and female he created them") as the basis of the church's teachings on sexuality, that document also asked for a reexamination of such matters as birth control, contraception, sterilization, illegitimacy, prostitution, and homosexuality. In addition, the report alluded to the need to focus on forgiveness, and it asked church members to reconsider both attitudes and laws relating to those ostracized by mainstream society for their sexual orientation. The report was especially significant because it addressed matters about which the church had long been silent. While still upholding traditional views about marriage as the standard for Christians, the convention report also inferred that the church should look at human sexuality through a broader lens than it had before.

Seven years later, professor Louie Crew and other Episcopalians organized an advocacy group designed to promote the concerns of lesbians and gays within the church. Known as Integrity, this organization, active at the 1976 General Convention, argued for the full and open acceptance of homosexual Christians. Integrity members helped influence the convention's adoption of two important resolutions: one, recognizing that "homosexual persons are children of God who have a full and equal claim with all other persons upon the love, acceptance, and pastoral concern and care of the Church"; and two, endorsing the idea that homosexuals are entitled to the same civil rights as other citizens.[3] Although those resolutions were overshadowed by the convention's even more controversial decision to approve the ordination of women to the priesthood, their implications were not lost on Paul Moore, the activist bishop of New York. In January 1977 Moore ordained Ellen Barrett, a lesbian and one of the original co-presidents of Integrity, to the priesthood. Moore's action brought forth a cry of outrage from many of his fellow bishops. Moore's critics soon helped fashion a pastoral letter that questioned the appropriateness of ordaining gays and lesbians and reaffirmed the traditional model of Christian marriage—positions with which the 1979 General Convention also expressed agreement.

Despite the bishops' statement, questions concerning the denomination's position on homosexuality (whether homosexuals ought to be ordained, and whether homosexual relationships should be blessed by the church) have been on the agenda of virtually every General Convention and meeting of the House of Bishops since the year of Barrett's ordination. Discussions over sexuality have become increasingly polarized in recent years, moreover, as Episcopalians have divided themselves into opposing and often hostile camps. A watershed was reached in 1996, however, when Walter Righter, the retired bishop of Iowa, was placed on trial for heresy. Righter was charged with violating his ordination vow to uphold the doctrines and laws of the Episcopal Church by ordaining an openly gay man to the diaconate in the diocese of Newark in 1990. The jury of eight bishops acquitted Righter of the charge of heresy because (they said) the Episcopal Church recognized no "core doctrines" that concerned the canonical status of non-celibate homosexuals in its midst. Developments at the 1997 General Convention further underscored the importance of that decision. The convention decreed that dioceses should offer health benefits to unmarried domestic partners, and it also came very close to authorizing the development of a rite for the blessing of same-sex unions. And, in an unprecedented move, the convention issued an apology to gays and lesbians for what it described as "years of rejection and maltreatment by the Church."[4] The 2000 General Convention, while defeating a resolution that would have authorized the development of a rite for same-sex unions, did recognize the existence of committed, monogamous, homosexual relationships.

～ The Anglican Communion

Despite the recent change of attitude toward homosexuality among many Episcopalians, not all Anglicans are in agreement with the policies of the church in the United States. Indeed, the Lambeth Conference of 1998 revealed that Episcopal leaders are radically out of step with their fellow bishops in other parts of the Anglican Communion, especially in third-world countries. Though admitting that homosexuals are members of the church and worthy of pastoral concern, the overwhelming majority of bishops at Lambeth declared that homosexual activity is incompatible with what the Bible teaches, and they advised against either ordaining gays and lesbians or blessing their relationships. The bishops further affirmed that faithfulness in marriage was the Christian ideal for sexual expression, and they urged those who did not wish to marry to refrain from sexual activity altogether.

Although some conservative Americans favored the Lambeth resolutions because they upheld traditional scriptural standards regarding sexuality, most Episcopal leaders openly disagreed with the position the conference took. Responding to the outrage expressed by gay activists in the Episcopal Church and the Church of England, nearly one hundred and fifty Anglican bishops (including sixty-five in the United States) pledged to continue to work for the full inclusion of gay and lesbian Christians in the life and ministry of their churches. The strongest supporters of the Lambeth sexuality resolution, on the other hand, were African and Asian bishops who believed in the literal interpretation of the Bible and in a strict understanding of sexual morality. These third-world bishops were determined to resist what they saw as the growing tendency in Europe and the United States to reject scripturally based moral principles in favor of an ethic based exclusively on individual sexual satisfaction.[5]

∼ Biblical Teachings

This insistence on the primacy of biblical teachings, however, raises questions about what the Bible actually says on the subject of homosexuality. A cursory perusal of the scriptures reveals that they say very little about this subject. According to one scholar, only seven passages—four in the Old Testament and three in the New Testament epistles—mention homosexuality.[6] That topic is not mentioned in the Ten Commandments, in the prophetic books of the Old Testament, or in the gospels. Jesus, in fact, seems to have been silent on it. And while Paul mentions homosexuality, his interest in it was minor in comparison to other sins (idolatry, contentiousness, and internecine strife, for example) practiced in the various Christian communities he visited during his missionary travels.

In the Old Testament, the creation story in the first two chapters of Genesis has often been cited as evidence that heterosexuality (along with marriage and procreation) is a central part of God's plan. Genesis also recounts the story of the destruction of Sodom and Gomorrah (Genesis 19:1-9). This is clearly the best known instance in the scriptures in which homosexuality is thought to be condemned, and indeed, the word "sodomy" has become a synonym for homosexual relations. Yet modern-day biblical scholars question whether the sin for which Sodom was destroyed was in fact homosexuality, since other references to Sodom in the Bible make no allusion to that idea. Some scholars even argue that, based on Jesus' words in the gospels (for example, Matthew 10:14-15 and Luke 10:10-12), the sin for which he thought Sodom had been destroyed was inhospitality, not homosexuality. In the New Testament, several Pauline letters refer to homosexuality, but while it is indisputable that Paul thought homosexual acts were wrong, he condemned them principally because he believed they were examples of pagan behavior. Furthermore, as L.

William Countryman observes, "homosexuality" is an entirely modern concept. The ancient Greeks and Romans assumed that human beings were essentially bisexual, and they expected people to feel sexual attraction to both their own and the opposite sex. Seen in this context, the activities that Paul disparages probably do not refer to modern notions of adult same-sex attraction, but to homosexual liaisons that were common in his day, namely, pederasty and male prostitution.[7]

∿ Church Teachings

Despite the ambiguity of the biblical record, everyone who weighs into this debate has to admit that the church's moral theologians have—until very recently, at least—declared homosexual acts to be sinful. That proscription has been predicated not only on the few biblical texts discussed above, but also on the philosophical concept known as "natural law." According to that idea, homosexual acts are unnatural because they violate the essential character of human sexuality: intercourse between a man and a woman for the purpose of begetting children. The first-century Jewish philosopher Philo, for example, condemned homosexual activity and intercourse with a menstruating woman with equal fervor: in his estimation, both represented a clear violation of the "law of nature."[8] A variant of this view was central to a document promulgated by the bishops of the Church of England in the early 1990s. Although the English bishops conceded that there is some genetic evidence for the existence of a "homophile orientation," they stated that the moral question about homosexuality concerns not its origins, but its ends. In their estimation, genital acts are definitive. Whenever those acts occur between people of the same sex—whether homosexual *desires* are natural or not—they do not fulfill the natural purpose of sexual intercourse and, hence, are morally wrong.[9]

～ The Current Debate

Now while it is not within the scope of this chapter to resolve the ongoing debate as to whether homosexuality is the result of "nature" or "nurture," suffice it to say that most scientific studies—as even the English bishops acknowledged—now point to some kind of genetic predisposition toward homosexuality. In other words, many intelligent people today hold the view that one does not "become" a homosexual because of the influence of family, neighborhood, or other social conditions. Sexual orientation, whether it is applied to heterosexuals or to homosexuals, is not a *choice*—any more than race or gender are. Both homosexuality and heterosexuality are morally neutral. We do not condemn heterosexual persons for *being* heterosexual, although we may well raise questions about how they express their sexuality. We decry inappropriate or immoral heterosexual *acts*, not the orientation of the actor. One of the major problems we face in the ongoing debate on human sexuality, however, is that there is no generally accepted norm for homosexuals. Although marriage is recognized as the best way for heterosexual Christians to express themselves sexually, society offers no corresponding ideal for lesbians and gays.

Despite the rancor with which the current debate is approached, human sexuality is hardly the first issue over which Episcopalians have found themselves seriously divided during the course of our history. Unlike other historic controversies, however, sexuality engages us at the most fundamental level of our being and raises disturbing questions both about our personal identities and about the nature of settled truth. For many believers today, the church's position on homosexuality has become a litmus test for all sorts of issues relative to the place of Christianity in the modern world. Moreover, because of an irrational fear of homosexuals, known as homophobia, gays and lesbians have been subject to ridicule, harassment, derision, and—as in the case of the brutal murder of Matthew Shepard, a gay student in Wyoming—acts of extreme violence. Indeed, some believe that bigotry against gays and lesbians is the last acceptable prejudice in contemporary American society.

Although reports from the 1998 Lambeth Conference suggested that all African Anglicans decried the existence of homosexuality and condemned those who engage in homosexual acts, it is important to note that Archbishop Desmond Tutu, clearly the best known of all African prelates, saw homosexuals in a very different light. Tutu made it clear that, for him, homophobia—like apartheid—is a justice issue. The bishops of the Province of South Africa also noted (in a statement released in March 1998) that the treatment of homosexuals is an urgent pastoral concern facing the church today. Despite centuries of mistreating and rejecting lesbians and gays, the bishops said, the church needs to repent of its misdeeds and ask forgiveness from the many homosexual people whom it has hurt. Just as listening to the experiences of racial minority groups has sensitized the church and disabused church members of the stereotypes that impede mutual understanding, so leaders in the churches of the Anglican Communion need—as the Lambeth resolution on sexuality itself suggested—to be attentive to the testimonies of gay and lesbian Christians. Church leaders must resist the temptation to attack homosexuals on the basis of simplistic interpretations of a few biblical texts.

Let me conclude with two additional observations. First, given the amount of emphasis that has been placed on the Bible in recent debates about homosexuality, would it not be wise to remember the mandate for inclusiveness that permeates virtually every page of the New Testament? Jesus embraced Samaritans, tax collectors, and lepers, and he scandalized the self-righteous Pharisees when he dined with outcasts. Jesus invariably reached out to people who had been shunned by those in positions of religious authority and privilege. "Unlovables" like Zacchaeus (Luke 19:1-10), the blind beggar Bartimeus (Mark 10:46-52), and the paralytic at the pool at Bethesda (John 5:2-9) were special beneficiaries of Jesus' compassion. Condemning lesbians and gays simply because of their sexual orientation is, therefore, not an acceptable option for anyone who believes in the Bible and who professes to be a Christian.

Second, I would like to suggest that, in seeking to discover a moral and theological framework within which the church can operate, we should turn to Richard Hooker, Anglican's chief apologist in the sixteenth century. It is Hooker to whom we are indebted for the "three-legged stool" of scripture, tradition, and reason on which the ethos and identity of Anglicanism rest. In his opening volume in The New Church's Teaching Series, James E. Griffiss observes that the genius of Hooker's theology is found in his desire to maintain continuity with traditions received from the past while accommodating the changes that new situations demand. Hooker's theological method requires, therefore, that the Bible does not stand alone.[10]

There is surely no issue in the church today that could benefit more from Hooker's approach than the debate over human sexuality. As we try to discern the mind of the church on this question, we must not fall into the trap of wresting "legs" from Hooker's "stool" and using them as weapons against our opponents. In the current discussion, some have shaken the scripture leg, pointing to the inerrancy of the Bible as the only possible Christian standard. Others, who regard revelation as a finite rather than a gradually evolving phenomenon, brandish the tradition leg. Appealing to scripture and tradition alone, the matter of human sexuality might well be settled. Both the Bible and the writings of theologians for all but the last few decades of the church's history have upheld a view of human sexuality that allows no room for the validity, integrity, and morality—much less the sanctity—of homosexual relationships.

However, in a denomination that values the power and authority of human intellect, it is time to allow reason to function as Hooker intended it—namely, as a means through which we may look at scripture and tradition in a new light, informed by insights derived from the sciences. It is also time to approach homosexual persons not as statistics or as "cases," but as fellow children of God. Indeed, our renewed understanding of theological ethics, which has enabled Episcopalians to listen to the voices of racial minorities, women, and other groups once denied a place at the table, should allow us to listen to the experiences of sexual minorities as well. And our pastoral heart, which has enabled us to feel the pain of divorced persons and to rethink traditional moral strictures, should be no less in evidence in the church's ministry to its gay and lesbian members. As the words of the baptismal covenant remind us, Christians are called to seek and serve Christ in *all* people, respecting their dignity and striving always for justice on their behalf.

Endnotes

∾ **Introduction: Christian Social Witness**
1. Kit and Frederica Konolige, *The Power of Their Glory: America's Ruling Class, the Episcopalians* (New York: Wyden Books, 1978).
2. Gardiner H. Shattuck, Jr., *Episcopalians and Race: Civil War to Civil Rights* (Lexington: University Press of Kentucky, 2000), 89.
3. Powel Mills Dawley, *The Episcopal Church and Its Work* (Greenwich, Conn.: Seabury, 1955), 234.

∾ **Chapter 1: The Bible**
1. Maria Harris, *Proclaim Jubilee! A Spirituality for the Twenty-first Century* (Louisville, Ky.: Westminster John Knox, 1996), 76.
2. Bruce V. Malchow, *Social Justice in the Hebrew Bible* (Collegeville, Minn.: Liturgical Press, 1996), 22.
3. Ibid., 22.
4. Harris, *Proclaim Jubilee!*, 21, 26.
5. Ibid., 76.
6. John R. Donahue, "Biblical Perspectives on Justice," in John C. Haughey, ed., *The Faith That Does Justice* (New York: Paulist Press, 1977), 68.

7. George V. Pixley and Clodovis Boff, *The Bible, the Church, and the Poor* (Maryknoll, N.Y.: Orbis, 1986), 20.

8. Liberation theologians, who write theology from the vantage point of the poor (as opposed to the privileged, who have dominated theological discourse for most of the history of the church), are staunch incarnationalists, and they believe that Holy Scripture continually reveals God's preference for the poor. See Pixley and Boff, *The Bible, the Church, and the Poor,* 53.

9. Michael Johnston, *Engaging the Word* (Cambridge, Mass.: Cowley, 1998), 76-77.

10. *The Hymnal 1982*, Hymn 633.

∾ Chapter Two: The Church of England

1. Kent White, "The Incarnation and Social Conditions," in Humphry Beevor, ed., *Catholic Sermons* (London: SPCK, 1932), 111.

2. James E. Griffiss, *The Anglican Vision* (Cambridge, Mass.: Cowley, 1997), 51.

3. Mark McIntosh, *Mysteries of Faith* (Cambridge, Mass.: Cowley, 2000), 103.

4. *The Oxford Dictionary of the Christian Church*, ed. F. L. Cross (Oxford: Oxford University Press, 1978), 696.

5. The reference is to a speech delivered by the Bishop of Zanzibar at the Anglo-Catholic Congress of 1923, cited in Griffiss, *Anglican Vision*, 52.

6. W. Norman Pittenger, *The Word Incarnate: A Study of the Doctrine of the Person of Christ* (London: James Nisbet, 1959), 177-78.

7. *The Hymnal 1982*, Hymn 528.

8. John S. Marshall, ed., *Hooker's Polity in Modern English* (Sewanee, Tenn.: University Press, 1948), 99.

9. Richard Hooker, "A Learned Sermon on the Nature of Pride," in W. S. Hill, ed., *Tractates and Sermons,*

Folger Library Edition of the Works of Richard Hooker, vol. 5 (Cambridge, Mass.: Belknap Press, 1990), 333.

10. John S. Marshall, *Hooker and the Anglican Tradition: An Historical and Theological Study of Hooker's* Ecclesiastical Polity (Sewanee, Tenn.: University Press, 1963), 121.

11. See Paul F. M. Zahl, *The Protestant Face of Anglicanism* (Grand Rapids, Mich.: Eerdmans, 1998).

12. *Oxford Dictionary of the Christian Church*, 486.

13. Ibid., 1467 (italics added).

14. E. R. Norman, *Church and Society in England 1770-1970: A Historical Study* (Oxford: Clarendon, 1976), 124-25.

15. William J. Wolf, ed., *The Spirit of Anglicanism: Hooker, Maurice, Temple* (Wilton, Conn.: Morehouse-Barlow, 1979), 59.

16. W. Merlin Davies, *An Introduction to F. D. Maurice's Theology* (London: SPCK, 1964), 33.

17. F. D. Maurice, *The Kingdom of Christ*, ed. Alec R. Vidler (London: SCM Press, 1958), 1:286-87, 330. Maurice's eucharistic theology is reflected, in part, in the words of a communion hymn: "Strengthen for service, Lord, the hands that holy things have taken" (*The Hymnal 1982*, Hymn 312).

18. Robert E. Hood, *Social Teachings in the Episcopal Church* (Harrisburg, Penn.: Morehouse, 1990), 41-43.

19. Edward Bouverie Pusey, "Sermons During the Season from Advent to Whitsuntide, 1848," in Geoffrey Rowell, *The Vision Glorious: Themes and Personalities of the Catholic Revival in Anglicanism* (Oxford: Oxford University Press, 1983), 82.

20. For a full discussion of this topic, see Michael Battle, *Reconciliation: The Ubuntu Theology of Desmond Tutu* (Cleveland, Ohio: Pilgrim, 1997).

21. William Temple, *Christianity and Social Order* (New York: Penguin, 1942), 17.

22. William Temple, *Citizen and Churchman* (London: Eyr and Spottiswood, 1947), 70.

23. *The Hymnal 1982*, Hymn 215.

~ **Chapter Three: The Episcopal Church**

1. Hood, *Social Teachings in the Episcopal Church*, 33.

2. This has certainly been true in matters relating to the church's black constituency—see Harold T. Lewis, *Yet With a Steady Beat: The African American Struggle for Recognition in the Episcopal Church* (Valley Forge, Penn.: Trinity Press International, 1996).

3. John M. Burgess, "The Role of ESCRU in the Life of the Church" (June 22, 1962), Records of the Episcopal Society for Cultural and Racial Unity, Archives of the Episcopal Church, Austin, Texas. See also David L. Holmes, *A Brief History of the Episcopal Church* (Valley Forge, Penn.: Trinity Press International, 1993), 80-82; and Shattuck, *Episcopalians and Race*, 9-10.

4. Cited in Joseph Blount Cheshire, *The Church in the Confederate States* (New York: Longmans, Green, 1912), 114.

5. Hood, *Social Teachings in the Episcopal Church*, 66.

6. For a fuller discussion of this period, see Shattuck, *Episcopalians and Race*, 7-29; and Lewis, *Yet With a Steady Beat*, 39-61.

7. *The Hymnal 1982*, Hymn 609.

8. *The Hymnal 1982*, Hymn 583.

9. Cited in Holmes, *Brief History of the Episcopal Church*, 126.

10. Henry F. May, *Protestant Churches and Industrial America* (New York: Harper, 1949), 186.

11. Warner R. Traynham, *Christian Faith in Black and White: A Primer in Theology from the Black Perspective* (Wakefield, Mass.: Parameter Press, 1973), 110.

12. Martin Luther King, Jr., "Nobel Prize Acceptance Speech," in James Melvin Washington, ed., *A Testament*

of Hope: The Essential Writings of Martin Luther King, Jr. (San Francisco: HarperSanFrancisco, 1986), 225–26.

13. Cited in Lewis, *Yet With a Steady Beat*, 150.

14. Hood, *Social Teachings in the Episcopal Church*, 65.

∽ **Chapter 4: Economic Justice**

1. James H. Cone, *God of the Oppressed* (Maryknoll, N.Y.: Orbis, 1997), 74–75.

2. Joerg Rieger, *Remember the Poor: The Challenge to Theology in the Twenty-First Century* (Harrisburg, Penn.: Trinity Press International, 1998), 155.

3. Ibid., 118.

4. Cone, *God of the Oppressed*, 72.

5. Gustavo Gutiérrez, *A Theology of Liberation: History, Politics, and Salvation*, rev. ed. (Maryknoll, N.Y.: Orbis, 1988), 143.

6. M. Douglas Meeks, *God the Economist: The Doctrine of God and Political Economy* (Minneapolis: Fortress, 1989), 23.

7. Ibid., 35.

8. "Debtor Nations Call for Justice, not Forgiveness," Anglican Communion News Service [ACNS] Press Release, no. LC045 (July 24, 1998).

9. "Lambeth Plenary Focuses on Issue of International Debt," ACNS Press Release, no. LC050 (July 26, 1998).

10. Ibid.

11. For quotation, see *Journal of the General Convention of the Protestant Episcopal Church* (1919), 508.

12. Norman Faramelli, Edward Rodman, and Anne Scheibner, "Seeking to Hear and to Heed in the Cities," in Clifford J. Green, ed., *Churches, Cities, and Human Community: Urban Ministry in the United States, 1945–1985* (Grand Rapids, Mich.: Eerdmans, 1996), 98.

13. Arnold Hamilton Maloney, "Whites Strive to Keep the Colored Race Divided," *Negro World* (June 1922).

14. C. Eric Lincoln and Lawrence H. Mamiya, *The Black Church in the African American Experience* (Durham, N. C.: Duke University Press, 1990), 241.

15. A full discussion of Messiah's outreach ministries is found in Nile Harper, *Urban Churches, Vital Signs: Beyond Charity Toward Justice* (Grand Rapids, Mich.: Eerdmans, 1999).

16. Richard L. Tolliver, "The African American Parish and Economic Development," *Anglican Theological Review* 77 (1995): 545-46.

17. The story of St. Edmund's community programs is found in Harper, *Urban Churches, Vital Signs*.

18. National Conference of Catholic Bishops, *Economic Justice for All: Pastoral Letter on Catholic Social Teaching and the U.S. Economy* (Washington, D.C.: U.S. Catholic Conference,1986), 1.

19. Faramelli, et al., "Seeking to Hear and to Heed," in *Churches, Cities, and Human Community*, 119.

20. "Remarks of Archbishop Njongonkulu Ndungane to the Lambeth Plenary on International Debt," ACNS Press Release, no. LC048 (July 24, 1998).

~ **Chapter 5: Race**

1. Ralph Ellison, *Invisible Man* (New York: Random House, 1952), 3.

2. Alexander Crummell, recently added to *Lesser Feasts and Fasts*, was in 1839 denied admission to the General Theological Seminary because of his race. He later pursued his theological studies instead in England at Queens College, Cambridge.

3. Harold T. Lewis, "The Parable of the Missing Church: A Lesson in Subtle Racism," *Anglican Theological Review* 81 (1999): 125-30.

4."*Other Sheep I Have": The Autobiography of Father Paul M. Washington* (Philadelphia: Temple University Press, 1994), 10-11. In the twentieth century, only four black clerics were appointed to serve as overseas missionaries of the Episcopal Church: Washington in Liberia, George Brandt in Botswana, Thomas Gibbs in the Virgin Islands, and the author in Honduras.

5. Lincoln and Mamiya, *Black Church in the African American Experience*, 1.

6. Samuel Wilberforce, *A History of the Protestant Episcopal Church in America* (London: J. Burns, 1846), 426.

7. J. Carleton Hayden, "Afro-Anglican Linkages 1701-1900: Ethiopia Shall Soon Stretch Out Her Hands Unto God," *Journal of Religious Thought* 44 (1987): 25.

8. To understand the reasons why racism exists in church and society today, we must first grasp how the ideology of American slavery required that black people be seen not even as second-class citizens, but as a subhuman species. According to Kortright Davis, "Blacks are a particular type of people who have the distinction of being the only ones in history whose claims of being human have been systematically called into question" (*Emancipation Still Comin': Explorations in Caribbean Emancipatory Theology* [Maryknoll, N.Y.: Orbis, 1990], 118). Our language, too, is reflective of such thinking. If a major corporation, for example, resolves to increase diversity in its workforce, it often announces that the company will seek "a qualified black man" to fill the position. When leading discussion groups on race, I sometimes ask the audience, "Have you ever heard the expression, 'qualified *white* man?'" After they invariably answer, "No," I explain that in our society "qualified white man" is considered a redundancy!

9. *The Hymnal 1940*, Hymn 254.

10. *Journal of the General Convention of the Protestant Episcopal Church* (1949), 164.

11. John Booty, *The Episcopal Church in Crisis* (Cambridge, Mass.: Cowley, 1988), 55-57.

12. *Journal of the General Convention of the Protestant Episcopal Church* (1955), 258-59.

13. Morgan Godwyn, "The Negro's and Indian's Advocate, Suing for the Admission to Their Church," in Robert W. Prichard, ed., *Readings from the History of the Episcopal Church* (Wilton, Conn.: Morehouse-Barlow, 1986), 8-9.

14. Holmes, *Brief History of the Episcopal Church*, 159.

15. Hood, *Social Teachings in the Episcopal Church*, 129.

～ Chapter 6: Gender

1. Peter J. Gomes, *The Good Book: Reading the Bible with Mind and Heart* (New York: Morrow, 1996), 122-23.

2. *Journal of the General Convention of the Protestant Episcopal Church* (1958), 345.

3. Pamela W. Darling, *New Wine: The Story of Women Transforming Leadership and Power in the Episcopal Church* (Cambridge, Mass.: Cowley, 1994), 30.

4. Mary Sudman Donovan, *A Different Call: Women's Ministries in the Episcopal Church, 1850-1920* (Wilton, Conn.: Morehouse-Barlow, 1986), 50.

5. Ibid., 88-90.

6. Rima Lunin Schultz, "Woman's Work and Woman's Calling in the Episcopal Church: Chicago, 1880-1989," in Catherine M. Prelinger, ed., *Episcopal Women: Gender, Spirituality, and Commitment in an American Mainline Denomination* (New York: Oxford University Press, 1992), 36-37.

7. *Journal of the General Convention of the Protestant Episcopal Church* (1913), 162.

8. Darling, *New Wine*, 54.

9. Ibid., 75-80.

10. Ibid., 92-93.

11.Voting "by orders" is a parliamentary procedure often used to make more difficult the passage of controversial resolutions at General Convention. Instead of a resolution's being passed by a simple majority of all deputies in the House of Deputies, it can be approved only when a majority of diocesan deputations in both orders—lay and clerical—vote in favor of it. If either the four lay or four clerical votes in each deputation are evenly divided (2-2), the vote of that divided deputation is counted as a *negative* vote. Thus, while the majority of individual deputies may well approve the passage of a resolution, that measure can still be defeated if it fails to carry a majority of deputations in both orders.

12. Darling, *New Wine*, 129.

13. Pauli Murray, *Pauli Murray: The Autobiography of a Black Activist, Feminist, Lawyer, Priest, and Poet* (Knoxville: University of Tennessee Press, 1989), 362.

14. Ibid., 371, 431.

～ **Chapter 7: Human Sexuality**

1. Timothy F. Sedgwick, "The Transformation of Sexuality and the Challenge of Conscience," in Charles Hefling, ed., *Our Selves, Our Souls and Bodies: Sexuality and the Household of God* (Cambridge, Mass.: Cowley, 1996), 27.

2. Ibid., 33.

3. *Journal of the General Convention of the Protestant Episcopal Church* (1976), C-109.

4. *Journal of the General Convention of the Protestant Episcopal Church* (1997), 278.

5. John L. Kater Jr., "Faithful Church, Plural World: Diversity at Lambeth 1998," *Anglican Theological Review* 81 (1999): 241.

6. Choon-Leong Seow, "Textual Orientation," in Robert L. Brawley, ed., *Biblical Ethics and Homosexuality:*

Listening to Scripture (Louisville, Ky.: Westminster John Knox, 1996), 26. The texts are Genesis 1:27-28 (and other aspects of the creation story in Genesis 1-2); Genesis 19:1-9; Leviticus 18:22; Leviticus 20:13; Romans 1:26-27; 1 Corinthians 6:9; and 1 Timothy 1:10.

7. L. William Countryman, *Dirt, Greed, and Sex: Sexual Ethics in the New Testament and Their Implications for Today* (Philadelphia: Fortress, 1988), 117-19.

8. Ibid., 62-63.

9. *Issues in Human Sexuality: A Statement by the House of Bishops of the General Synod of the Church of England* (Harrisburg, Penn.: Morehouse, 1991), 31-41.

10. Griffiss, *Anglican Vision*, 26-27.

Resources

∼ The Bible

A very good place to begin one's reading about social witness in the Bible is Maria Harris's *Proclaim Jubilee! A Spirituality for the Twenty-first Century* (Westminster John Knox, 1996), which examines the Old Testament idea of jubilee and considers how that concept might be applied to the present day. Bruce Malchow's *Social Justice in the Hebrew Bible: What Is New and What Is Old* (Liturgical Press, 1996) also provides a fine introduction to the Old Testament teachings about social justice. *The Bible, the Church, and the Poor* by George Pixley and Clodovis Boff (Orbis, 1986) sets out the biblical basis of God's "option for the poor." As this book argues, the Old Testament reveals God as a liberator of the oppressed, while the New Testament demonstrates God's fundamental solidarity with the lowly.

Ched Myers's *Binding the Strong Man: A Political Reading of Mark's Story of Jesus* (Orbis, 1988) is a convincing effort by an activist trained in the biblical academy to apply a liberation reading of scripture to Mark's gospel. Myers offers an exhaustive commentary that invites readers to look at the social and economic world in which Mark lived and to recognize the political character of all theological discourse.

In *The Good Book: Reading the Bible with Mind and Heart* (Morrow, 1996), Peter Gomes, pastor of Harvard University's Memorial Church, presents a compelling account of what the Bible means for contemporary Christians. Writing for a popular rather than an academic audience, Gomes attempts to reclaim the scriptures from those who would misuse them to alienate and exclude people on the margins of society.

~ The Church of England

For an excellent overview of the history, theology, and ethos of the Anglican Communion, see *The Study of Anglicanism*, edited by Stephen Sykes and John Booty (SPCK/Fortress, 1988). This collection brings together a series of essays about all aspects of Anglicanism, including a helpful section on "Anglicanism in Practice," in which the most pertinent article is Paul Elmen's "Anglican Morality."

The two classic texts on social witness in the Church of England are F. D. Maurice's *The Kingdom of Christ* (originally published in 1838) and William Temple's *Christianity and Social Order* (Penguin, 1942). Maurice Reckitt discusses the linkage between these great Anglican thinkers in his book *Maurice to Temple: A Century of the Social Movement in the Church of England* (Faber and Faber, 1947). Paul Phillips's *A Kingdom on Earth: Anglo-American Social Christianity, 1880-1940* (Pennsylvania State University Press, 1996) provides a useful modern history of the Social Gospel and Christian Socialist movements in Britain, Canada, and the United States. Finally, Michael Battle's *Reconciliation: The Ubuntu Theology of Desmond Tutu* (Pilgrim, 1997) examines the important contributions of that twentieth-century leader to the Anglican social tradition.

⁓ The Episcopal Church

Stephen Bayne's *Christian Living* (Seabury, 1957), which was published as a volume in the original Church's Teaching Series, offers a useful analysis of Episcopal social teachings in the mid-twentieth century. And for an insightful and more critical examination of the history of the church's witness on war and peace, race, economics, and sexuality, see Robert Hood's *Social Teachings in the Episcopal Church* (Morehouse, 1990).

Three excellent books published in the past ten years describe the overall history of Anglicanism in the United States: Robert Prichard's *A History of the Episcopal Church* (Morehouse, 1991); David Holmes's *A Brief History of the Episcopal Church* (Trinity Press International, 1993); and *Documents of Witness*, a collection of primary sources edited by Don Armentrout and Robert Slocum (Church Hymnal, 1994). Focused principally on the 1960s and 1970s, John Booty's *The Episcopal Church in Crisis* (Cowley, 1988) interprets a critical period in American history in which Episcopalians dealt with a number of pressing social issues.

In addition to these scholarly treatments of social witness, two recent biographical studies illuminate the theological views of Episcopalians immersed in the social struggles of the twentieth century. Bill Wylie Kellermann edited an excellent volume on the social witness of lawyer and theologian William Stringfellow, *Keeper of the Word: Selected Writings of William Stringfellow* (Eerdmans, 1994), while Paul Moore's autobiography, *Presences* (Cowley, 1997), describes his ministry as an advocate for the poor and oppressed both in American cities and overseas.

~ Economic Justice

Strongly influenced by Marxism, the theology of liberation that emerged in Latin America in the 1960s envisioned salvation primarily in political and economic terms. One of its leading exponents, Gustavo Gutiérrez of Peru, argues that the Bible becomes relevant only when it speaks to the situation of human beings in the world. His most important works are collected in *Gustavo Gutiérrez: Essential Writings*, edited by James Nickoloff (Fortress, 1996). African American theologian James Cone's *God of the Oppressed* (Orbis, 1977) argues that any analysis of the gospels that does not begin with God's liberation of the oppressed cannot claim to be Christian. Following the lead of thinkers such as Gutiérrez and Cone, Joerg Rieger's *Remember the Poor: The Challenge to Theology in the Twenty-First Century* (Trinity Press International, 1998) seeks to create a new paradigm for religious and spiritual reflection: "theology from below."

Examining the issues related to economic justice from a practical point of view, Nile Harper's *Urban Churches, Vital Signs: Beyond Charity Toward Justice* (Eerdmans, 1999) describes some of the actual ways in which local churches are now ministering in urban neighborhoods in the United States. Another valuable book is M. Douglas Meeks's *God the Economist: The Doctrine of God and Political Economy* (Fortress, 1989), which reconceptualizes the Christian understanding of God so that the church can wrestle more faithfully with the serious economic issues of the present day.

Sharon Welch's *Communities of Resistance and Solidarity: A Feminist Theology of Liberation* (Orbis,

1985) offers a political interpretation of the Christian faith from the perspective of a white, middle-class American woman who has a double identity as both oppressor and oppressed.

∿ Race

C. Eric Lincoln and Lawrence Mamiya's *The Black Church in the African American Experience* (Duke University Press, 1990) provides essential background reading on the role of the black churches in American religious life, while Peter Paris's *The Social Teaching of the Black Churches* (Fortress, 1985) is an excellent introduction to the political and social ethics of African American Christians. Three recent studies examine the generally troubled history of race relations in the Episcopal Church: Harold Lewis's *Yet With a Steady Beat: The African American Struggle for Recognition in the Episcopal Church* (Trinity Press International, 1996); Gardiner H. Shattuck's *Episcopalians and Race: Civil War to Civil Rights* (University Press of Kentucky, 2000), and Michael Beary's *Black Bishop: Edward T. Demby and the Struggle for Racial Equality in the Episcopal Church* (University of Illinois Press, 2001). Paul Washington's *"Other Sheep I Have": The Autobiography of Father Paul M. Washington* (Temple University Press, 1994) is a revealing memoir of the ministry of one of the most influential African American priests of the twentieth century.

James Cone's *A Black Theology of Liberation* (Lippincott, 1970) was a ground-breaking exploration of the idea that political, social, and economic justice for African Americans is intimately related to the gospel of Jesus Christ. Cone's writings inspired a host of other works of black theology, including two important books written by Anglicans: Warner

Traynham's *Christian Faith in Black and White: A Primer in Theology from the Black Perspective* (Parameter Press, 1973) and Kortright Davis's *Emancipation Still Comin': Explorations in Caribbean Emancipatory Theology* (Orbis, 1990). Cheryl Sanders's *Empowerment Ethics for a Liberated People: A Path to African American Social Transformation* (Fortress, 1995) employs the insights of black liberation theology to construct a moral framework in which African American Christians can make ethical decisions that affect society.

Although most studies of race and the Episcopal Church have focused on African Americans, Owanah Anderson's *400 Years: Anglican/Episcopal Mission Among American Indians* (Forward Movement Publications, 1997) offers a helpful history of the church's work with Native Americans.

～ Gender

Three books provide essential information about the history of women in the Episcopal Church: Mary Donovan's *A Different Call: Women's Ministries in the Episcopal Church, 1850-1920* (Wilton, Morehouse-Barlow, 1986), which focuses on the contributions of lay women; Pamela W. Darling's *New Wine: The Story of Women Transforming Leadership and Power in the Episcopal Church* (Cowley, 1994), which traces the history of the Woman's Auxiliary and women deputies to General Convention and examines the movement for the ordination of women; and *Episcopal Women: Gender, Spirituality, and Commitment in an American Mainline Denomination*, edited by Catherine Prelinger (Oxford University Press, 1992), which contains articles on a variety of topics by scholars in both sociology and religious history.

Joanna Gillespie's *Women Speak: Of God, Congregations, and Change* (Trinity Press International, 1995) is an exceptional study of the perceptions and insights of ordinary women in congregations across the United States, while *Pauli Murray: The Autobiography of a Black Activist, Feminist, Lawyer, Priest, and Poet* (University of Tennessee Press, 1989) recounts the experiences of the first African American woman ordained a priest in the Episcopal Church.

Womanspirit Rising: A Feminist Reader in Religion, edited by Carol Christ and Judith Plaskow (Harper & Row, 1979) is a collection of some of the earliest writings of the feminist movement within the church. It includes essays by theologians such as Rosemary Radford Ruether, Mary Daly, and Elisabeth Schüssler Fiorenza. Delores Williams's *Sisters in the Wilderness: The Challenge of Womanist God-Talk* (Orbis, 1993) seeks to move beyond black theology (written from the perspective of African American men) and feminist theology (written from the perspective of privileged white women) in order to formulate a "womanist" theology based on the experiences of women of color.

∾ Sexuality

L. William Countryman's *Dirt, Greed, and Sex: Sexual Ethics in the New Testament and Their Implications for Today* (Fortress, 1988) reassesses some familiar New Testament texts in order to shed important light on modern controversies about Christian sexual ethics. Phyllis Trible's *God and the Rhetoric of Sexuality* (Fortress, 1978) is a path-breaking effort to reinterpret the scriptures through the hermeneutic of sexuality. And *Biblical Ethics and Homosexuality: Listening to Scripture* edited by Robert L. Brawley (Westminster John Knox, 1996) challenges church people to heed the multiplicity of voices that are engaged in debates regarding sexual behavior today.

For an understanding of the role of gays and lesbians in the Christian community over the centuries, the works of historian John Boswell—*Christianity, Social Tolerance, and Homosexuality* (University of Chicago Press, 1980) and *Same-Sex Unions in Premodern Europe* (Villard, 1994)—are absolutely essential reading.

Our Selves, Our Souls and Bodies: Sexuality and the Household of God, a collection of essays edited by theologian Charles Hefling (Cowley, 1996), addresses the recent turmoil in the Episcopal Church over sexuality, especially questions about the blessing of same-sex unions and the ordination of lesbians and gays. The various contributors to that volume consider the debate about sexuality from biblical, theological, ethical, and pastoral perspectives.

Finally, Carter Heyward's *Touching Our Strength: The Erotic as Power and the Love of God* (Harper & Row, 1989) represents an attempt to give voice to women and men who experience sexuality as a liberating resource. According to Heyward, it is important for Christians to lay to rest the church's traditional, dualistic outlook on the relationship between sexuality and spirituality.

Questions for Group Discussion

~ **Chapter 1: The Bible**

1. Turn to the baptismal covenant beginning on page 304 of *The Book of Common Prayer* and read it through, focusing particularly on the question, "Will you seek and serve Christ in all persons, loving your neighbor as yourself?" Now think back upon the churches you have grown up in, as well as the church you belong to today. How has this promise been carried out with regard to the mission and ministry of the parishes you have known? In what concrete ways has this promise been associated with outreach?

2. The author speaks about the provision of a year of jubilee in the Old Testament, in which the land was allowed to lie fallow so that "the poor of your people may eat." The practice of jubilee also meant the cancellation and forgiveness of outstanding debts. What diocesan or parish programs in the Episcopal Church do you think have fulfilled the intent of the jubilee year? What actions could you envision the church taking today to keep the spirit of jubilee?

~ Chapter 2: The Church of England

1. The opening quotation by Christian Socialist Frederick Denison Maurice states that all who enter the kingdom of God become "interested in all its relations, members, circumstances.... In this highest sense, the churchman must be a politician." In what ways does this belief of Maurice's about church and politics mirror your own? How does it differ?

2. It is an important belief in Anglicanism that a strong connection exists between the Incarnation—the fact that God became a human being in Jesus—and social action. How do you understand this? How does a strong belief that the church is, in the words of theologian James E. Griffiss, "called to witness to the Incarnate Christ in all the conditions of human existence" inform our social witness?

~ Chapter 3: The Episcopal Church

1. In chapter one we were reminded that although we come to the Bible as a resource for ethics, far too often "we make up our social values as we go along ... and then we impose them on the Bible." The views held about slavery before and during the American Civil War are a good example of this practice, with both abolitionists and slaveholders citing different texts of scripture to bolster their case. What contemporary examples can you think of?

2. The Episcopal Church was the only mainline Protestant denomination that did not split over the Civil War, but stayed together in a spirit of unity and fellowship. More recently divisions over the place of women and of gays and lesbians in the church have threatened to divide it. What price do you think the

church pays when it places fellowship over protest, unity over justice?

ᴖ Chapter 4: Economic Justice

1. In this chapter Harold Lewis cites a number of biblical texts that seem to support God's "preferential option for the poor," such as "the tax collectors and the prostitutes are going into the kingdom of God ahead of you" (Matthew 21:31). In what ways do you find this theology just or unjust? In what ways would you have to change your theological outlook in order to accept this idea?

2. Frederick Denison Maurice wrote, "We have been dosing our people with religion when what they want is not this but the living God." Here Maurice seems to suggest that "the living God" is urgently concerned with material as well as spiritual welfare. If this is true, in what ways do you think that your own parish church offers its members "the living God"?

ᴖ Chapter 5: Race

1. In the previous chapter the author argues that the invention and celebration of the concept of multiculturalism has grown out of our discomfort with the reality of racism in everyday life. In what ways do you think this is true? In what ways do you disagree with his statement?

2. Lewis notes that many marginalized groups in the church have been relegated to being invisible to those in the dominant culture. In what ways have you experienced this to be true? How can individuals and groups who have been ignored because of race "become visible"? In what ways do you think the

church is called to be an advocate for those on the margins?

~ Chapter 6: Gender

1. Think back on the women who held commanding roles in the church you grew up in, whether Episcopal or some other denomination. Did they inhabit a "separate sphere"? What are some of the stories and recollections that come to mind? How have your memories of these women affected the way you see the roles of women in your own parish today?

2. Lewis describes the struggles of African Americans and of women to assume authority in the church as similar. The church, like society at large, maintained that both groups inhabited "separate but equal" spheres. Do you find these parallels valid or not, and why? Are there similar groups in the church or society today that are treated as "separate but equal"?

~ Chapter 7: Human Sexuality

1. Why do you think that the issue of sexuality arouses such strong controversies in the church, even stronger than those over prayer book revision and women's ordination?

2. Why should a chapter on sexuality and sexual orientation be included in a book on Christian social witness?

Cowley Publications is a ministry of the Society of St. John the Evangelist, a religious community for men in the Episcopal Church. Emerging from the Society's tradition of prayer, theological reflection, and diversity of mission, the press is centered in the rich heritage of the Anglican Communion.

Cowley Publications seeks to provide books, audio cassettes, and other resources for the ongoing theological exploration and spiritual development of the Episcopal Church and others in the body of Christ. To this end, it is dedicated to developing a new generation of theological writers, encouraging them to produce timely, creative, and stimulating publications of excellence, and making these publications available widely, reaching both clergy and lay persons.